CONTENTS

Fashion Forecasting, 3rd Edition

Fashion used to come from one source at a time, be it the street, the runways, or the entertainment business. The interesting thing about today is that influences come from high and low— everything from couture to Target.

—Michael Kors

FAIRCHILD BOOKS
CUSTOM PUBLICATION

Fashion History & Terminology

FASH126

ISBN: 978-1-60901-764-4

Humber College

Originally Published in:

Fashion Forecasting, 3rd Edition

EVELYN L BRANNON

Fairchild Books
an imprint of Bloomsbury Publishing Inc. 2013

Library of Congress Catalog Number: 2012944357
ISBN: 978-1-60901-764-4
Printed in The United States of America

Page references refer to those found in the original publications:

Fashion Forecasting, 3rd Edition
Evelyn L. Brannon
Copyright © 2010 Fairchild Books, A Division of Condé Nast Publications
ISBN: 978-1-56367-820-2

1
THE FASHION FORECASTING PROCESS

OBJECTIVES
- Understand the multifaceted character of fashion
- Analyze the trajectory of fashion change
- Identify the concept of Zeitgeist, or spirit of the times, as a framework for understanding and interpreting fashion change
- Understand the breadth and depth of the forecasting process
- Identify the role of forecasting in the textile and apparel industries

Trend Chasers—Who, What, Where, When, Why, and How

Meteorologists who study the formation and behavior of tornadoes are called storm chasers. They position themselves in the geographic location most likely to spawn these violent but short-lived weather events. Then, with skill, knowledge about storm behavior, perseverance, and a little luck, they locate and investigate the phenomenon. They transmit their findings to other meteorologists and, eventually, to the public.

Like the storm chasers, trend chasers locate the spawning ground of trends and use their skill and knowledge to identify emerging concepts. Trend chasers transmit their findings to other forecasters, product developers, marketers, and the press, setting off the chain reaction that people call fashion. The result is a continuous flow of products with new styling, novel decoration, and innovative uses.

Trend chasers work in many kinds of firms—for designers, advertising agencies, fiber producers, trade organizations, retail chains, and apparel brands. However, their job titles rarely include variations on the word *forecaster*. Instead, these executives have job titles that range from manager of trend merchandising to creative director, and their backgrounds are varied ("The next," 2003).

- Roseann Forde, Fordecasting. Forde studied to be a buyer, but found her calling when she became the manager of a fabric library. She was Global Fashion Director for INVISTA (formerly DuPont) for a decade before starting her own trend forecasting agency.
- Kathryn Novakovic, Cotton Incorporated. Novakovic wanted to start a business making hand-knit sweaters, but instead majored in textile science at college. Later she worked as a production engineer for a fabric company and moved on to the design and production staff of a major apparel brand, before becoming a trend forecaster.

One thing all forecasters have in common is frequent travel. Forde makes quarterly trips to London, Paris, and Milan. Novakovic browses flea markets in London and researches color in the Scandinavian countries. Color forecasting dates from the early twentieth century and trend merchandising from the 1950s. For decades trendspotting meant reporting on the runways and what stylish people wore in Europe. Today finding trends means looking worldwide and the search is incomplete without analyzing their market potential (Zimmerman, 2008) (Figure 1.1).

Forecasters also work in trend analysis firms that consult with companies in apparel, cosmetics, and interior design. Each firm develops a distinctive approach (Loyer, 2002). Compare how two Paris firms characterize their mission on their Web sites:

- Nelly Rodi looks for "new consumer behavior patterns" and applies "creative intuition" to shape insights for clients.
- Peclers Paris analyzes trend evolution from inception to confirmation and serves as "innovation catalysts" for clients.

Trend analysis firms publish books to illustrate their forecasts about 18 months ahead of the fashion season. The books include color chips, textile samples, fashion sketches, and photographs to illustrate trends. Increasingly the trend books are being supplemented or replaced with Web sites offering video, photographs, downloadable sketches, color swatches, print and fabric designs, and software tools. These subscription-only, business-to-business sites provide real-time trend forecasting. For example, Stylesight (www.stylesight.com) has a library of three million images—not just clothes but also stores, inspiration shots like graffiti, and streetwear from around the world. Images are tagged and indexed for easy retrieval. A yearly subscription to the site costs $15,000 and allows access to twenty users in an apparel firm. Other forecasting services offer similar services (see Resource Pointers). The new sites substitute for the work formerly done by fashion scouts (although firms still use fashion scouts who travel the world to find fashion inspiration) (Miller, 2008).

Not all forecasters live in the fashion capitals. Many retailers and manufacturers base forecasters in their corporate offices, close to buying and product development teams. By traveling to fashion centers, covering trade shows, seeking out emerging retail concepts, and tracking consumer behavior, these professionals bring inspiration and direction to companies with a fashion-based strategy.

Whatever their title or hunting strategy, trend chasers enable companies to execute a strategy based on timing. Called **strategic windows,** this strategy involves timing the firm's product offerings to the customer's readiness and willingness to accept and adopt the products (Abell, 1978).

FORECASTING DEFINED

Fashion **forecasting** has been compared to chasing the future with a butterfly net (Gardner, 1995). But spotting trends is not that difficult for people who immerse themselves in popular culture and trade news. Forecasters pluck emerging trends out of public information by becoming sensitive to directional signals that others miss. Faith Popcorn, the founder and CEO of the marketing consulting company BrainReserve and one of the first forecasters to gain name recognition in the media, calls this "brailing the culture"—looking for the new, the fresh, and the innovative, and then analyzing the whys behind it (1991).

Forecasters vary in the methods they use, but all are looking for an apparatus that helps them predict the mood, behavior, and buying habits of the consumer. Because trends signal the emerging needs, wants, and aspirations of the consumer, astute manufacturers and retailers capitalize on their potential for turning a profit.

Figure 1.1.
Finding trends
means looking world-
wide. Fashion weeks
in sites from Berlin to
Bali and Hong Kong
to São Paulo offer fore-
casters a window
on what's new. Sydney
hosts the runways of
Australian Fashion Week.
(*WWD*, Courtesy of
Fairchild Publications)

Figure 1.2.
Forecasters use the tools
of the trade—color, textures,
and photographs—to explain
the forecast to clients.
(© Image Source)

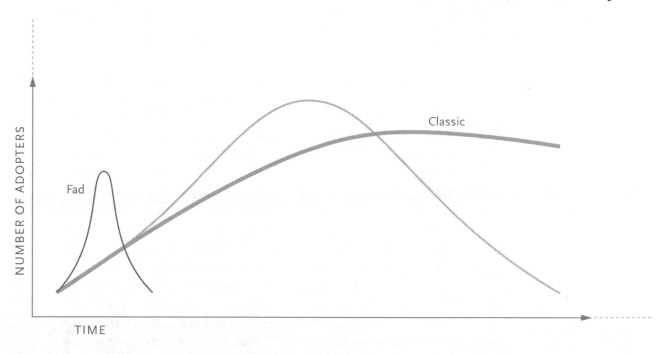

NUMBER OF ADOPTERS

Fad

Classic

TIME

Figure 1.3.
Short-lived fads versus classic clothes that stay in style for longer periods can be visualized by graphing their popularity and duration.

Forecasting is not magic practiced by a talented few with a gift of seeing the future. It is a creative process that can be understood, practiced, and applied by anyone who has been introduced to the tools (Figure 1.2). A professional does not proceed by rule of thumb or trial and error but by mastery of the theory and practice of the field. Forecasting provides a way for executives to expand their thinking about change, anticipate the future, and project the likely outcomes (Levenbach & Cleary, 1981).

Executives use forecasting as input for planning. Marketing managers position products in the marketplace using short- and long-term forecasts. Planners of competitive strategies use forecasting techniques to look at market share and the position of competitors in the marketplace. Product developers, merchandisers, and production managers use the short-term trend forecasts of color, textiles, and style direction to shape collections.

Visualization and Forecasting
In the narrowest sense, forecasting attempts to project past trends into the future. A **trend**

is a transitory increase or decrease over time (Makridakis, 1990). Some trends have lasted for millennia—human population growth, for example. But all trends have the potential to eventually slow down and decline.

Although attention is showered on the most exciting and extreme runway fashions, the mechanisms of fashion change work in the background to create patterns familiar to the most experienced fashion watchers. **Visualization** helps forecasters understand and communicate the movement of fashion and project future directions. Three of the most familiar patterns are fashion curves, the pendulum swing, and the fashion cycle.

- Fashion curves—Fashion trends are usually classified by duration and penetration, visualized as curves with time on the bottom axis and consumer adoption rates on the vertical axis (see Chapter 2 for details on this kind of analysis). In this way it is easy to show the difference between the shortest trends, called **fads,** and the longest trends, called **classics** (Figure 1.3).

- Pendulum swing—**Pendulum swing** refers to the periodic movement of fashion between extremes—for example, fluctuations between long and short hemlines, fitted and oversized silhouettes, and dressed-up and casual looks. These swings may take decades or occur in just one fashion season. Visualize the swing from power dressing of the late 1980s to the relaxed dress codes of the late 1990s. In the early years of the next decade, forecasters began anticipating a swing back. The runway shows for fall 2008 featured classic looks, a return to tailoring, and a more controlled aesthetic. American fashion designer Michael Kors argued that the return to more conservative styles was "the opposite of trying so hard to look undone," which he claimed women in their twenties found stale (La Ferla, 2008a). Men's fashions showed the same pendulum swing with the return of the tie after more than a decade of neglect during the era of "Casual Friday." No longer required, the tie became a style statement for men in their twenties and thirties who redefined it to express their creative side (Colman, 2007).
- Fashion cycles—**Cycles** have a fixed, regular periodicity. Economic and business cycles have been proposed but are considered controversial. Variations in the length and depth of "cycles" make the term a misnomer. No fixed, regularly recurring cycles have been identified and used to accurately predict the next cycle in business or fashion (the failure to identify a regular recurring fashion cycle is discussed in Chapter 3). Instead, it is more accurate to call recurring patterns a **long-wave phenomenon** (Fischer, 1996). Long-wave refers to any entity (e.g., prices or styles) with movement that rises and falls with differences in duration and magnitude, velocity, and momentum across time periods. This wave model is reflective of movement in social spheres, including fashion. Popular in the hippie era of the 1960s and 1970s, handicrafts like knitting, embroidery, patchwork, and quilting fell out of style. The very word *craft* carried a meaning opposite to "fashionable" for decades. Inspired by museum exhibitions like the Gee's Bend quilters of Alabama and vintage fashion, designers began showing "handmades" on the runways in the mid-2000s and needlecrafts of all kinds became fashionable again. "Craft" became synonymous with "chic" when sophisticated styles were executed in intricate patterns, unusual yarns, and vintage fabrics. The most talented craftspeople market online on sites like Etsy.com, a showcase for ideas that is monitored by forecasters and apparel designers (La Ferla, 2007b).

Steps in Developing a Forecast

Forecasting consists of tools and techniques applied systematically. Just as important are human judgment and interpretation (Levenbach & Cleary, 1981). The steps in developing a forecast are:

Step 1	Identify the basic facts about past trends and forecasts.
Step 2	Determine the causes of change in the past.
Step 3	Determine the differences between past forecasts and actual behavior.
Step 4	Determine the factors likely to affect trends in the future.
Step 5	Apply forecasting tools and techniques, paying attention to issues of accuracy and reliability.

Step 6   Follow the forecast continually to determine reasons for significant deviations from expectations.

Step 7   Revise the forecast when necessary.

A trend forecast should identify the source, underlying pattern, direction, and tempo of the trend.

The most valuable currencies in today's competitive climate are information and learning. Information is a business asset that can be managed like any other quality or talent. Executive decisions are enhanced in an information-rich environment. However, obtaining information is only the first step in the process of organizing, analyzing, understanding, and learning from it. Information is easy to find but difficult to sift, frame, and integrate so that learning can take place. Forecasting is the process that translates information into a form that allows learning to occur.

FORECASTING SPECIALTIES

Forecasting is more than just attending runway shows and picking out potential trends that can be knocked off at lower prices (although that is part of it). It is a process that spans shifts in color and styles, changes in lifestyles and buying patterns, and different ways of doing business. What appears to be near-random activity is in fact a process of negotiation between the fashion industry and the consumer, and among the various segments in the supply-side chain.

By education and training, executives develop a specialty, one that restricts their view of information. These executives tend to restrict themselves to only a narrow scan of information generated within a specialty or within an industry segment. In doing so, they risk developing tunnel vision by focusing on information internal to the company and industry to the exclusion of the broader cultural perspective. Tunnel vision reduces the flexibility that is so essential for decision making under conditions of high-velocity change.

Even though apparel experts must become experts in an information domain bounded by their placement on the supply chain, product category, or job description, all apparel executives share the same problem—how to make the right product, introduce it at the right time, distribute it in the right channels, and capture the attention of the right consumers. When specialists talk only to each other or talk to others in technical jargon, the chance to collaborate on solutions is squandered. Collaborative forecasting within a company and among companies in partnership encourages communication across domain boundaries.

Long-term forecasting (five years or more) is a way to explore possible futures and to build a shared vision of an organization's direction and development. A compelling vision draws people toward a preferred future. **Short-term forecasting** (one year ahead) involves periodic monitoring of the long-term vision and revisions as circumstances dictate and acts to coordinate the operations of a company within the context of the industry and the marketplace. Forecasting keeps the momentum going because it forces a perspective of the future on the day-to-day business decisions.

● ● ● ACTIVITY 1.1. Visual Directory

Look for examples of fads, classics, and styles that are recycled from past eras, as well as signs of pendulum swing in the current fashion season. Use fashion magazines and Web sites such as www.style.com or www.Firstview. com to locate the images. Then, use the pictures to define these fashion terms in a visual way. Continue to locate visual examples of the terms in this book and use them to create an illustrated fashion dictionary.

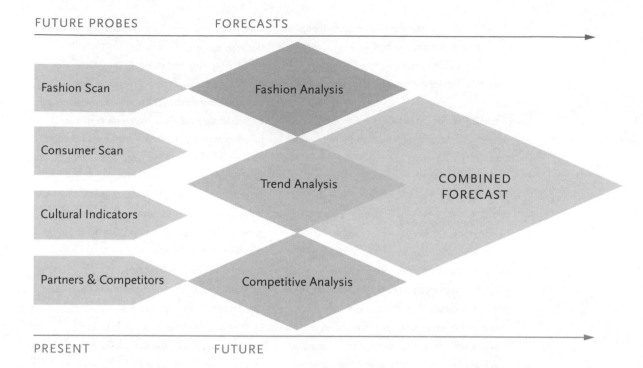

FUTURE PROBES   FORECASTS

Fashion Scan

Consumer Scan

Cultural Indicators

Partners & Competitors

Fashion Analysis

Trend Analysis

COMBINED FORECAST

Competitive Analysis

PRESENT   FUTURE

The focus of this book is on managing information as a corporate asset, an asset that can be managed like any other. Executives balance on a point in the present. Their decisions are supported by past experience— fashion history, sales history, and traditional ways of doing business. To keep their balance, executives need a window on the future—new innovations, cultural change, and alternative ways to do business. **Environmental scanning** opens that window on the future.

Executives gather useful external information when they scan a daily newspaper, watch TV news, listen to the radio while commuting to work, chat with people at a dinner party, and log on to the Internet. The difference between information gathered in this informal way and environmental scanning is a more systematic approach and use of information management tools. The building blocks of such a system are presented as chapters in this book (Figure 1.4).

Fashion Scan

Fashion professionals eagerly follow the latest fashion news to spot emerging fashion and lifestyle trends. Environmental scanning for trends includes:

- Traveling to the fashion capitals (New York, Paris, Milan, and London) and to other trendsetting spots to observe firsthand.
- Scanning print, broadcast, and online sources for clues.
- Networking with people in creative fields such as the arts, architecture, interior design, cosmetics, and entertainment.

Supplementing the individual's effort, forecasters and trend analysis firms gather information and present summaries in trend books, newsletters, and seminars.

Specialists (whether forecasters or apparel executives) focus on color, textiles, or style

Figure 1.4.
Fashion forecasting requires a balanced view that seeks out the newest styles breaking on the cultural edge (fashion scan), shifts in the cultural environment (trend analysis), and marketing climate (competitive analysis).

forecasting—each of which works on its own schedule, internal logic, and insider expertise. The first three chapters in this book discuss the internal logic of fashion forecasting. Insider expertise is explored in chapters on each specialty (Chapters 5, 6, and 7). Sales forecasting examines sales history for trend indications and projects demand for the coming season based on insiders' judgment and expertise (Chapter 7). Together these forecasting disciplines are the domain of the fashion scan.

Consumer Scan

Consumer segmentation attempts to identify clusters of people who share characteristics, usually some combination of demographics, lifestyle, attitudes, and behavior. Consumers who share characteristics are called **cohorts**—the basic unit of consumer research. For example, the consumer segment of working women can be subdivided by categories such as occupation, age, marital status, number of children, ethnicity, or other characteristics. Working women with many shared characteristics are a cohort who are likely to shop and purchase in similar ways. Consumer research uses various data gathering methods (e.g., focus groups, surveys, and observation) to explore consumers' preferences and behavior. By linking the subsegments with price points, brands, shopping behavior, and style preferences, an executive can determine which consumers are likely to respond to the company's offerings—the **target market**.

Consumer research is an important part of fashion forecasting today. Evaluation of **point-of-sale (POS) data** tells the retailer and manufacturer what sold when and at what price. But POS data cannot explain why consumers made a purchase or what consumer needs, wants, and desires went unmet by the available assortment. Insights provided by consumer research help executives develop short-term forecasts that guide product development, merchandising, marketing, and promotion. In this book, Chapter 2 discusses consumer segmentation in more detail and Chapter 8 discusses data-gathering methods and the interpretation of findings.

Consulting firms, market research organizations, advertising agencies, the government, and individual companies are constantly conducting consumer research. Whereas this research is usually proprietary (belongs to the organization that funded it), summaries are often available in trade publications or other print, broadcast, and online sources. Journalists, sociologists, psychologists, and others write about their observations of consumer culture and hypothesize about its underlying structure. Locating these sources using environmental scanning helps the apparel executive to identify shifts in consumer lifestyles, preferences, and behavior that impact store design, merchandise assortments, and fashion promotion.

Fashion Analysis

Combined, the fashion scan and consumer scan provide input for fashion analysis—putting together the puzzle of what is likely to happen next. Fashion is really a dialogue among the creative industries—fashion, interior design, the arts, and entertainment—that propose innovations and consumers who decide what to adopt or reject. As one forecaster put it, "Nothing will succeed in fashion if the public is not ready for it" (O'Neill, 1989). Fashion analysis brings together the expertise of a fashion insider and insights on consumer behavior to provide support for executive decisions in the supply chain from fiber to fabric to apparel manufacturing to retailing.

Social and Economic Trends

The shift to green marketing (positioning products, their manufacturing processes, and distribution as sensitive to environmental concerns) and a consumer resistant to following trends are manifestations of deep cultural changes in society. The fashion story is part of larger shifts in the culture, including the fragmentation of the marketplace. Fashion forecasting requires a wide scan to encompass cultural, economic, and technology issues that have an impact on consumer preferences and spending. Some forecasters and forecasting firms focus on large-scale shifts in cultural indicators. These **megatrends** cross industry lines because they involve shifts in lifestyles, reflect changes in generational cohorts, or mirror cycles in the economy. Trends of this magnitude may be felt over the period of a decade, from the first time that they surface to the time that they influence purchasing decisions on a mass scale. For the fashion industry and related categories such as interiors and automobile styling, monitoring these cultural indicators is essential for strategic planning and to provide a backdrop to short-term forecasts. Environmental scanning allows any executive to monitor cultural indicators that alter the business environment and change consumers' purchasing behavior. (Chapter 4 introduces forecasters who specialize in the long view, and discusses their methods of gathering and interpreting data.)

Trend Analysis

Drawing on fashion and consumer scans, and on identification of social and economic trends, trend analysis detects short- and long-term trends that affect business prospects. Trends start as experiments, self-expression, and reactions to changing circumstances. Many vanish almost as soon as they are created but some gain adherents and build momentum. When they are recognized by the gatekeepers of fashion—designers, journalists, merchants, and forecasters—the trends start to appear in media coverage. Trend analysis looks at the interaction of shifts in fashion, consumer lifestyles, and culture.

Competitive Analysis

Space in stores is finite. Apparel competes for consumers' attention and dollars with many other alternatives, including electronics and entertainment. To be competitive in such a business environment, companies must observe competing firms through regular tracking of key information. Over time this effort allows a company to benchmark its activities against competitors and to develop "what if" scenarios about competitor initiatives. Whether it is called competitive analysis, competitive information, or competitive intelligence, business survival and growth depends on using public sources to monitor the business activities of partners and competitors. New businesses depend on this kind of information in the start-up stage; established businesses use it to help them scout out new markets; and large corporations treat it as input for senior managers coordinating activities across markets and product lines. Competitive analysis is a continuous, long-term project that uses many of the same research and analysis strategies as other forms of forecasting (see Chapter 11).

Integrated Forecasting

No organization should rely too heavily on a single forecasting discipline or on an individual forecaster for decision support. The information environment is so rich, no one person can possibly locate and interpret all the signs and signals across multiple time horizons. Yet little effort or attention has been given to integrating information across forecasting specialties—fashion trends, shifts in consumer culture, megatrends, and competitive analysis. Information is only the raw material. It must be processed, spun, and woven into a forecast. A team approach to forecasting means continuous information sharing between functional groups with the goal of increasing the quality of the forecast. A multifaceted outlook benefits a company by providing both a better general picture of developments and a more fine-grained interpretation.

The best forecasts blend quantitative and qualitative components, the wide view of cultural indicators and the close focus of sales forecasting, and short-range and long-range time scales. Interpretations must be keyed to specific consumer segments and a competitive niche. Strategies that work for teens experimenting with identity and style, those that work for mainstream working people, and those for active retirees are very different. Change produces different effects according to the target consumer and the industry segment.

Intelligent use of forecasting keeps an executive from focusing narrowly on a specialty instead of how that specialty integrates with others in the decision-making chain. Integrated forecasting provides a combined forecast targeted to consumer preferences, a company's marketing niche, the competitive environment, and cultural shifts. Forecasts do not provide "the answer." Instead, forecasting opens a window on the possibilities and probabilities of the future.

Discovering the Zeitgeist

Fashion historians contend that fashion is a reflection of the times in which it is created and worn. Fashion responds to whatever is modern—that is, to the spirit of the times or the **Zeitgeist** (a German word used to describe the general cultural climate of a specific period in time). According to Blumer (1969), individuals in large numbers choose among competing styles those that click or connect with the spirit of the times. This **collective selection** forms a feedback loop between the fashion industry and the consumer, a feedback loop that can be read in sales figures. The problem with this concept in terms of forecasting is that it offers little advance warning. Only **fast fashion** firms—those set up to deliver new styles in weeks instead of months—are able to capitalize on the fast-changing trends as they are revealed in the data. Other companies act only after fashion converges on the styles symbolic of the times.

All cultural components respond to the spirit of the times. The power of the Zeitgeist

● ● ● ACTIVITY 1.2. Megatrends

Megatrends cross industry lines, involve shifts in lifestyle, or mirror economic cycles. The effects of these trends will be felt for a decade or more. Gather four or five friends and brainstorm a list of ten megatrends. Start with those that are currently being discussed in newspapers, magazines, and online (environmental issues, alternative energy sources, increasing longevity, etc.). Look for those beginning to emerge—what issues are making a difference in lifestyles? Discuss what impact these forces will have on the fashion industry. Move from the general (environmental concerns) to the specific (sustainable agriculture and industrial waste). Will these megatrends be opportunities or threats to current business practices? Step into the role of a forecaster and write a news article on the top five megatrends that will change the fashion industry in the next ten years.

is its ability to coordinate across product categories. Fashion and cuisine exhibit the same trends and cycles. In the mid-1980s, the newest trend in cuisine was Tex-Mex, but that was replaced by Cajun only a few years later. Once all "fashionable" sandwiches were served on pita bread, a few years later it was the croissant, after that it was multigrain peasant-style bread, and then wraps and panini. Fashion affects all product categories—food, sports, architecture, interiors, and automobile styling. Soccer was once an obscure sport in the United States, whereas today it is an avid passion of many Americans. Sports such as bicycle racing and snowboarding were once the province of a small cadre of participants. Today they are covered on television sports channels and the functional clothing of participants has been adapted to mass fashion. Toys, avocations, pastimes, and play all respond to the same cultural currents that fashion does.

Media not only report on the culture, they are shaped by it. Watching network television was all-important until the coming of hundreds of cable and satellite channels, the Web, and gaming systems pushed the networks off the cultural front burner. The Internet and gaming systems changed the entertainment landscape. Magazines are like any other product; they have natural life cycles connected to the spirit of the times. New magazines start up to reach new audiences. Existing magazines reinvent or refresh their look and their focus in response to the spirit of the times. Often this process involves a change in editors. New editors replace old ones because they have a vision, one that is in touch with the times, and they can shape the magazine to reflect this change.

DEFINING FASHION

In the simplest terms, **fashion** is a style that is popular in the present or a set of trends that have been accepted by a wide audience. Fashion is a complex phenomenon from psychological, sociological, cultural, or commercial points of view.

Fashion as a Social and Psychological Response

Defining fashion means dealing with dualities because clothing simultaneously conceals and reveals the body and the self. Clothing choices express personal style and individuality but also serve to manipulate a person's public image to fit situations and the expectations of others. The engine of fashion is sparked by the dual goals of imitation and differentiation, of fitting in and standing out, of following the leader and being distinctive (Flugel, 1930; Simmel, 1904). Human ambivalence—conflicting and contradictory yearnings—finds an outlet in a capitalist marketplace as "appearance-modifying" goods. Through a process of negotiation between elements of the fashion industry and between the fashion industry and the consumer, ambiguous styles become accepted as fashionable (Kaiser, Nagasawa, & Hutton, 1995). Duality exists even in the buying of fashion because the process is both cognitively challenging (as when people evaluate price and value) and emotionally arousing (as when people react positively or negatively to the symbolic meaning in the products) (Brannon, 1993).

Fashion as Popular Culture

Defining fashion means operating within the domain of popular culture. Unlike high culture (fine art, classical music, and great literature), popular culture often seems trivial and transient.

Popular culture invites skepticism because it sometimes seems extreme and frivolous. For the same reasons, it is difficult to take fashion seriously. Fashion change is never entirely arbitrary, but ugly things are sometimes in vogue (Laver, 1937; Simmel, 1904). Most people invest their time, interest, and dollars in popular culture. The study of popular culture—the content and people's relationship to that content—has attracted the attention of scientists and scholars. Serious anthropologists, psychologists, and sociologists have written about fashion and theorized about its mechanisms of change.

Fashion as Change

Defining fashion as change captures the charm of novelty, the responsiveness to the spirit of the times, and the pull of historical continuity (Blumer, 1969; Simmel, 1904). Fashion is not a phenomenon restricted to apparel. It is present in the design of automobiles and architecture, the shifting popularity of cuisine, the development of technology, and the buzzwords of business management strategies. Every few years a new management strategy is touted as a breakthrough only to be replaced by another one a few years later. The World Wide Web was once an information network for scientists; now it reaches into offices and homes everywhere. Understanding fashion helps explain how these transformations happen.

Fashion as Universal Phenomenon

By the mid-fifteenth century, the French duchy of Burgundy became the center of fashion for a number of reasons. It was a crossroads of international trade with exposure to foreign styles. It had the beginnings of a fashion trade in materials, ideas, and artisans, and the members of the court desired to display wealth through elaborate costumes. Finally, Burgundy had a new style made visible by its duke and duchess. The style—a long, lean silhouette in black cloth with fur—was copied by aristocrats from other parts of Europe, establishing fashion as part of the lifestyle of the elite (Rubinstein, 2001). The excitement of fashion can apply to any area of life. In the 1630s, the tulip, an exotic import from central Asia, became the focus of desire. Wild speculation among the normally sober Dutch people drove the price up until a single rare bulb could cost as much as a house (Dash, 1999). Many examples across cultures and time periods illustrate that fashion is not restricted to any era or group. Fashion is the natural outcome of markets and consumers' wish for expression.

Fashion as a Transfer of Meaning

Meaning exists in the cultural environment. Designers, marketers, and the press transfer the meaning to a consumer product and increase its visibility. The consumer collects meaning out of the marketplace in the form of goods and constructs his or her own personal world (McCracken, 1988b). Not all products catch the attention of or find favor with consumers. Some meanings are rejected initially and are then taken up later. Some meanings are recycled over and over. Obsolescence is designed into the process. Fashion in its many guises plays a constant role in the evolving cultural environment. As Simmel said at the beginning of the twentieth century, "The very character of fashion demands that it should be exercised at one time only by a portion of the given group, the great majority being merely on the road to adopting it" (Simmel, 1904, p. 138).

Fashion as an Economic Stimulus

More than an abstract concept, fashion is an economic force. A wit, writing in *The New Yorker*, summed up the issue, "If clothes can not be relied on to wear out fast enough, something must be found that will wear out faster; that something is what we call fashion" (Gopnik, 1994). **Planned obsolescence** powers the economic engine of fashion. Wearing clothes until they wear out or wearing the secondhand clothes of more fickle buyers are acceptable strategies for dressing, but they omit the pleasure in new clothes and the novelty in new looks. Creating fashion goods requires the ability to mix aesthetic concerns and market mindfulness—that is, mass-produced fashion is the product of negotiation within and between the segments that make up the fashion industry (Davis, 1991).

Fashion and Gender Differences

Where apparel is concerned, men and women have not been playing on the same field. The modern men's suit began its evolution with a move away from decoration in the late 1780s during the post–French Revolution period. A split arose between the design and the manufacturing modes of men's and women's clothing beginning around 1820. By the mid-1800s, the prototype of the modern men's suit—matching pieces, a sack coat, simple and undecorated, designed for ease and action—had evolved. Women's clothes continued as colorful, ornamented, and restrictive (Hollander, 1994).

Men had rejected the social distinctiveness of dress in favor of "occupational" clothing with similarity in cut, proportion, and design (Flugel, 1930). Women, in a relatively weaker social position than men, used fashion as a field where they could vent their "individual prominence" and "personal conspicuousness" (Simmel, 1904). By the 1930s, fashion commentators were seeing a change—the breakdown of social hierarchies and the "ever-increasing socialization of women" (Flugel, 1930; Laver, 1937). These commentators began asking if these changes in the lifestyles and economic status of women would lead to the same reduction in clothes competition that had occurred among men. Fashion's future may bring reconciliation between the sexes with men having more access to color, ornament, and self-expression and women having less reliance on extraneous accessories, painful footwear, and constricting styles.

But fashion itself will continue to be available to all—for example, wristbands started as functional (to wipe sweat) and ended up as fashion for professional and college football players. Some players wear them high on the arm because with "all sorts of biceps and triceps busting out of there, it's a good look" (Branch, 2008). Some players wear fat two-inch wristbands, other cut them down for a thin look, a few wear two on each arm. Worn in the crook of the elbow or above (one player wears his over the sleeve on his shirt), wristbands have "no benefit from a performance standpoint, it's purely a fashion statement"—a fashion that has trickled down to middle school players (Branch, 2008).

NYSTROM'S FRAMEWORK FOR OBSERVING THE ZEITGEIST

What factors should the forecaster monitor? What external factors shape the spirit of the times? In 1928, Nystrom attempted to list factors that guide and influence the character and direction of fashion. His list still provides a framework for observing the Zeitgeist.

Dominating Events

Nystrom listed three kinds of dominating events: (1) significant occurrences such as war, the death of world leaders, and world fairs; (2) art vogues (the Russian Ballet and modern art in his day); and (3) accidental events (the discovery of the tomb of Tutankhamen in the 1920s). Historical examples such as the effect of pop, op, and psychedelic art on the fashions of the 1960s and 1970s extend Nystrom's analysis on the relationship between dress and art. Although world fairs no longer serve to set trends, other international events still pull in huge audiences. One such event is the Academy Awards ceremony with its celebrity fashion parade (Figure 1.5). Another is the influence of the Olympic Games on activewear for athletes and on casual wear for the mainstream consumer. An updated list of significant occurrences would include the end of the Cold War; the 1990s bull market on the stock exchange; Internet culture; the terrorist attacks on September 11, 2001, followed by military action in Afghanistan and Iraq; and the economic downturn in the United States beginning in late 2007. Lynch and Strauss (2007) propose performance as an instigator of fashion change whether the performance is by professionals (rock concerts, film, the red carpet, runway shows, or sports events) or through the mini-dramas of consumer stylists enacting a role. Fashion is not merely a reflection of the spirit of the times but part of its creation (Vinken, 2005).

● ● ● ACTIVITY 1.3. Discovering the Zeitgeist

Use Nystrom's framework to map the spirit of the times. Because each market segment will have its cultural identity within the cultural environment, try mapping the dominating events, ideals, social groups, attitudes, and technology for your own generational cohort group. How important does an event have to be to affect multiple cohorts? What does this suggest in relationship to product development and marketing? How are such maps useful to forecasters?

Dominating Ideals

Nystrom listed dominating ideals such as patriotism and the Greek ideal of classical beauty. An updated list would include ideals of multiculturalism, environmental and humanitarian issues, equality of men and women, and the connection among fitness, beauty, and youthfulness. The ideal of a multicultural society is not new in the United States, but it is being reshaped by the changing demographics of color within the population. Census figures show the Hispanic and Asian populations growing much faster than the nation's population as a whole. Some cities such as Baltimore and Detroit are becoming predominately African American; others such as San Antonio and Miami, predominately Hispanic. Asian influence is becoming stronger in cities such as Los Angeles, San Francisco, and New York. Because some of these cities are also important as style centers and as the starting points for trends, the impact on American fashion could be considerable.

Dominating Social Groups

Nystrom identified the dominating social groups as those with wealth, power, and leadership positions. Although the groups themselves would have changed, the criteria still apply to today's culture. Today, the power of celebrities in popularizing fashion trends can hardly be overemphasized. Stars in the music world are directional for younger customers, actors for the older customer (Kletter, 2003). Designer Narciso Rodriguez explains, "From a designer's perspective, each house represents a certain style or aesthetic—a look that has its own following. That's where a designer's power lies. It's not to say that designers don't influence fashion today, but I would imagine that music, performers, and actors have much

Figure 1.5.
Cate Blanchett's appearance at the Cannes Film Festival in an organza gown tells a color story (pink updated to salmon), a styling story (pleats and ruffles for dimension and texture), and an accessory story, and evokes a romantic mood—all with potential for trendsetting. (*WWD*, Courtesy of Fairchild Publications)

Figure 1.6.
Tam's design for
Hewlett-Packard—
a pared-down computer
notebook that is
functional, fun,
and fashionable.
(*WWD*, Courtesy of
Fairchild Publications)

more impact on the way people might dress, especially younger people. They are just much more visible to the mainstream population" (Wilson, 2003). Celebrities as presented through the multiple media channels—music videos, movies, TV series, interview programs, photographs in magazines and newspapers, and on Web sites—have become the highly visible and highly influential "new" elite.

Dominating Attitude

Nystrom's list must be extended to capture today's spirit of the times. Add to the list the dominating attitude of the times. The engine of fashion, the interplay between an individual's desire to fit in and to stand out, between imitation and differentiation, imprints the Zeitgeist (Brenninkmeyer, 1963). When the desire for differentiation is the dominant attitude in an era, new fashions arise, the changes are revolutionary, and the pace of fashion change is swift. The flapper era in the 1920s and Youthquake in the 1960s are examples of eras when the dominant attitude was differentiation. When social conformity

and imitation is the dominant attitude, fashion innovation slows down, the changes are evolutionary, and the pace of fashion slows down. The depressed 1930s, conforming 1950s, and dominance of casual styles beginning in the 1990s are such eras.

Dominating Technology

Today more than ever, Nystrom's list must be expanded to include the dominating technology of the times. When he was writing in the late 1920s, the harnessing of the atom, the space race, the power of television, and advent of the computer were all in the future. Today, technology is deeply intertwined in everyday life, especially in the realms of communication, entertainment, and computers. Cell phones, digital media players, GPS, and wireless connectivity make wearable technology an essential fashion accessory. Vivienne Tam designed a "digital clutch"—a pared-down notebook computer (weighing about a pound) with a colorful floral cover that made it a fun and fashionable accessory for the woman on the go (Corcoran, 2008d) (Figure 1.6).

Technology imprints not only the Zeitgeist but also the production methods. Without computers and rapid worldwide communication, quick response strategies and global apparel production would not be possible. Instant information exchange, computer technology, robotics, and automation are driving the paradigms of production on a mass scale and production of customized products for a market of one (mass customization).

Together, the dominating events, ideals, social groups, attitudes, and technology exemplify and influence the spirit of the times. Together they illuminate the structure of society with fashion illustrating variations on the cultural theme (Brenninkmeyer, 1963).

FORECASTER'S TOOLBOX: SEEING THE BIG PICTURE

A problem for forecasters is the difficulty in recognizing the spirit of the times while living in them. Retrospect allows the distinguishing characteristics of an era to become clear. Although there are some limits on newness in fashion—the shape of the human body, cultural theme of the times, and production technology available—there is still an enormous range of possibilities for experimentation. A fashion era can be characterized by:

- A designer's signature style—Halston in the 1970s, Christian Lacroix in the 1980s, Tom Ford in the 1990s, Marc Jacobs for the 2000s.
- A style leader—Jacqueline Kennedy in the early 1960s, Prada in the 2000s.
- A fashion look—the flapper of the 1920s, Cardin's and Courrèges' space-age short white dresses and boots in the mid-1960s, the 1977 "Annie Hall" look.
- A bohemian element—the Beats, the hippies, hip-hop.
- A market segment—the middle class in the 1950s, the youth movement in the 1960s, tweens in the 2000s.
- A celebrity icon—Clara Bow, the "It Girl" in the 1920s; Madonna, the "Material Girl" in the early 1980s; the *Sex in the City* stars in the 2000s.
- A model—Jean Shrimpton and Twiggy in the 1960s, Lauren Hutton and Christie Brinkley in the 1970s, the supermodels of the 1980s, Kate Moss in the 1990s, Gisele Bündchen in the 2000s.
- A fiber or fabric—Chanel's jersey, the polyester of the 1970s, Lycra in the late 1990s, organic cotton in the 2000s.

The silhouette changes with the times but so does the figure underneath. The tall, athletic Gibson girl gave way to the boyish flapper, the superfeminine sex goddess Marilyn Monroe was replaced by the reed-thin flower child, and the waif was replaced by the powerful, toned physique of female action stars. The ideals of beauty are just as malleable as the fashions (Danielson, 1989).

Whereas others merely participate in fashion change, forecasters attempt to understand the process, trace the evolution, and recognize the patterns. To do this, they must be participants, but they must also be spectators interpreting what they observe. The Zeitgeist is an expression of modernity, of the current state of culture, of the incipient and unarticulated tastes of the consuming public. Forecasters monitoring the Zeitgeist pay special attention to:

- Style interactions among apparel, cuisine, sports, architecture, interior design, automobile design and innovation, toys, avocations, pastimes, and play because all these fields respond to the same cultural currents.
- The content of media, the celebrities covered in the media, and the members of the press who decide what stories to cover.
- The events, ideals, social groups, attitudes, and technology that characterize the spirit of the times.

These cultural patterns define the present. Even slight shifts in these patterns act as directional signposts to the future.

FASHION DIRECTIONS

To look forward, a forecaster must have an image of the past—the way styles responded to and were shaped by the spirit of the times. Prognosticators at the turn of the twentieth century looked forward with an optimism buoyed by the success of the Industrial Revolution. They had faith that technology would create a bright, prosperous future. As with all forecasts, there were hits and misses (Leland, 2000). One educator wrote of homes connected by cameras and telephones so that the occupants could see around the world from their living room—a dream clearly realized with television and the Internet. An economist predicted that women would have more control over the purse strings and that men would adopt an ornamented look including tights—a vision that foresaw the arc that would take women from gaining the vote to entering the workforce in huge numbers, but only glimpsed changes that would loosen the rules of appropriateness for both sexes.

Forecasts are always vulnerable to the unexpected event or the unanticipated outcome. The optimistic view of technology at the turn of the twentieth century was shaken with the sinking of the *Titanic* in 1912, the symbol of technological achievement that proved all too fragile. World War I opened occupational doors for women who became nurses, office workers, and drivers, a situation that was repeated in World War II when women became factory workers and pilots, roles formerly reserved for men. World War II galvanized U.S. manufacturing, laying the foundation for post-war prosperity.

The marketplace is shaped by constant negotiation between the apparel industry and consumers over which styles represent the spirit of the times. It is not only the styles that change but also the marketplace dynamics. Looking back over the last century reveals the changes in the marketplace that will affect the future.

Shift from Appropriateness to "Anything Goes"

A woman, recalling the way she dressed for a day out in New York City in the summer of 1929, says that the ensemble began with a full set of underwear including a full-length slip and stockings, and finished with gloves and a hat. Today summer attire for a young woman in the same city might be shorts, tank top, and rubber flip-flops (Trebay, 2002). The strict social rules governing fashion ended in the mid-1960s. Gone were the traditions of no white shoes after Labor Day, no patent leather in the winter, no suede in the summer, velvet and taffeta only between Thanksgiving and New Year's Eve, and shoes matching handbags. Instead fashion professionals and consumers took a more permissive approach relying only on their eye to decide what looked right (Turk, 1989).

Where designer clothes in the 1950s looked as finished on the inside as the outside, by the 1990s clothing went from unconstructed to deconstructed—raveled edges, ragged, wrinkled, and faded on both sides. Replacing worn-out, bedraggled clothing with crisply new versions was once a principle driver for shopping. By agreeing that "anything goes" in terms of fashion and appropriateness, the fashion industry removed the incentive to update wardrobes and disrupted its own fashion cycles (Agins, 1995).

Shift from Fashion Seasons to Seasonless Dressing

Changing seasons once marked the fashion calendar for stores and consumers—fall, winter, spring, summer. The universality of environmental controls in building and transportation, changes in rules of appropriateness, and new fibers and fabrics made seasonless dressing possible. This shift was reinforced by volatile weather sometimes attributed to global warming—which doesn't mean warmer weather overall but more unpredictable weather. As one outerwear manufacturer put it, "I have been in this industry for 40 years, and during that time, we always knew it got cold in December and stayed that way through January and February. . . . Now, it's a crap shoot." In fact, a government panel found that the length of seasons had changed over a 50-year span—spring began arriving earlier and fall later, taking two weeks off the coldest period. Some large companies added a climatologist (sometimes known as "climate merchant") to their design team to help time shipments of season-specific garments (Barbaro, 2007b). The overall changing weather patterns reinforced the shift to seasonless fabrics and styles, removing the incentive for consumers to replace their wardrobe according to the changing seasons.

The change from definite fashion seasons to seasonless has the potential to revolutionize the marketplace. As Beppe Modenese, the founding father of Milan Fashion Week, sees it, "You can't have everyone showing four times a year to present . . . the same fabrics at the same weight. The fashion system must adapt to the reality that there is no strong difference between summer and winter anymore" (Trebay, 2007).

Shift from Fashion Experts to Consumer Opinion

Miniskirts in the 1960s, bell-bottom jeans in the 1970s, and power-shoulder suits in the 1980s—fashion once consisted of clear directional signals about what was "In" and "Out" and the desire to be "In" still motivated shopping (Pressler, 1995). By the early1970s, a women's magazine could declare in bold type: "Fashion is going out of fashion" ("Creative," 1971). The reasons listed included a rejection of the image of beautiful people who wear the latest thing in favor of an expanded definition of beauty and individuality—a shift from "what's in" to "what works."

Selling women's wear and menswear depends on the connection between the consumer's self-image and the narrative presented by the designer or brand. But consumers lose faith in the message when the narrative doesn't jibe with lifestyle aspirations (Trebay, 2003). This occurred in the mid-1980s, when the fashion industry pushed youthful fashions just when women entering the workforce in large numbers needed conservative work clothes—the women's sportswear market collapsed ("From stupidity,"1988). Designers, merchants, and the press lost credibility as style guides. One fashion commentator summed up the situation: "In fashion . . . we have witnessed the abdication of the experts. Everyone's opinion matters now, and no one's opinion matters any more than anyone else's" (Brubach, 1994).

The abdication of fashion leadership by the experts—designers, merchants, and journalists—led to an alienation among grassroots consumers who demoted fashion's importance on their shopping priority list. Those still placing a high priority on fashion as recreation (and re-creation) kept an eye on fashion news scripted by the fashion press and on Web sites where consumers dialogue with each other about styles and trends, as well as on fashion blogs where a self-appointed "expert" provides commentary. Other sites are completely consumer controlled: At Threadless.com anyone can submit designs that are voted into production by users who then can order the resulting products (Walker, 2007). A report on the WWD/DNR CEO Summit concluded: "Providers of goods and services will have to scramble to meet the needs of an increasingly educated, tech-empowered and self-service oriented consumer who will no longer wait to be 'sold' by a biased source" ("Outlook," 2008).

The Emergence of No-Fashion

"Dress for the job you want," the mantra of the mainstream, was grounded in the idea of upward mobility. In the early 1990s a "counter-fashion ethic" based on price, value, and a casual lifestyle emerged with the "grunge look." Originating in Seattle, Washington, grunge was a look, a variation of rock-and-roll, and an attitude—an unsexy, non-style featuring long hair, flannel shirts, and wool caps. Initially the look was more popular in the press than with customers, but hip-hop fashion—sweat clothes, cargo pants, athletic jerseys, and designer sneakers—carried on the dress-down philosophy. "Casual Fridays"—a shift from traditional corporate dressing to casual at least one day a week—moved dressing down from the street to the workplace. Casual became a lifestyle that extended to home furnishings, entertaining, and exercise. Even the trend on television programming toward reality shows played a part in legitimizing the no-fashion aesthetic. According to one designer, "Watching a reality TV show just enforces the notion that it is OK to wear anything, while high fashion to them seems like it is becoming more elitist" (Wilson, 2003). By the early 2000s forecasters identified the saturation of dressing down as a signal that the pendulum would swing back to something less "scruffy" (Jones, 2002). After a decade of dressing down, the news in both men's and women's fashions was not a "return to dressing up" but a cleaner, more pulled-together look that crossed boundaries between work and leisure. Tailored clothing borrowed details from sportswear, used softer fabrics, and less structure to create a look that could go to the office or dress up jeans (Thomas, 2007) (Figure 1.7).

Emergence of Cheap Chic

Over time retailers trained consumers to wait for markdowns before buying. Constant markdowns and markdowns early in the season upset the existing relationship between consumers and stores. Gone was the stigma of wearing cheap clothes and shoppers became less loyal to a brand or a designer and more focused on finding a bargain (Wilson, 2003).

During the same time period, price for mainstream fashion plummeted while prices for luxury goods inflated. Price deflation was caused mainly by the shifting of apparel production to countries with cheap labor. The change set up price competition among specialty chains, department stores, mass merchants such as Kmart and Wal-Mart, and fast-fashion firms. Eventually the question became "How low can prices go?" Bud Konheim, CEO of Nicole Miller, said, "I think we've exploited all the countries on earth for people who really want to work for nothing." When consumers view price as a deciding factor rather than desire, then the fashion industry has lost a central driver for fashion purchasing (Wilson, 2008). Costs of production offshore could increase with higher energy expenditures, making it harder to compete on price alone. Although price will always be an important consideration, consumers may modify their selection process to include other considerations such as environmental impact, humanitarian issues, and the reputation of the producing country.

Figure 1.7.
The menswear pendulum swings back to tailored clothes but with a softer, less constructed approach. (*WWD*, Courtesy of Fairchild Publications)

Power of Fashion Trends Dissipates

Today trends are not as broadly influential as they once were. When Yves Saint Laurent introduced his 1977 collection based on Russian themes, every product category and price point took part in the "folkloric" look. As forecaster David Wolfe commented, "The sort of creative ideas that used to be are now just flashes-in-the-pan. They come and go very quickly. . . . Today trends are little snapshots of style, not the big picture" (Schneiderman, 2001).

Time lags between the introduction of an innovation and its availability worked to the advantage of the industry. It allowed time to explain the innovation and increase its visibility and desirability. The less adventurous consumer who makes up the majority of the market needed that time to become familiar with the innovation before seeking to purchase it. And companies needed time to source and produce the new look as it trickled through the marketplace. Today those time lags have all but disappeared. Trends showcased on the runway can appear in moderate-priced stores before designer labels can deliver the look to high-priced boutiques. If a new style is simultaneously available at all levels of retail from department stores to specialty chains to mass merchants, there is less time to make money on the trend ("Direction," 1999).

Fragmentation in the marketplace also helped diminish the power of trends. The fashion industry itself became "too diffuse, with too many separate points of view, for anyone to pay the attention one once did" (Horyn, 2003). Similar to the music industry, the fashion industry had a few superstars, a few rising stars, and many others whose names were barely known even to insiders. How can reporters (much less the consumer) locate a core when "fashion has exploded into 1,000 tiny particles of style"?

When consumers changed the way they shopped—buying basics and replacement items as needed, purchasing fashion looks for immediate wear—it became more difficult for apparel companies to figure out which trends would be in and for how long, given a product development cycle of almost a year. To adjust to these changes, apparel companies cut their development schedule and moved the process closer to the store delivery dates (Larson, 2003).

Trends, once the motivation for shopping, can die before they reach the store. As one retail buyer put it, "You don't have enough time to create volume. By the time it gets onto the floor, kids are already tired [of it]." According to a retail analyst, trends now have a life span of 8 to 12 weeks instead of 5 months or more as they did in the late-1990s (D'Innocenzio, 2001). Trends that do catch on tend to influence a specific consumer segment. Without a time lag to introduce, explain, and promote the trend, it fails to spread to other consumer categories. For fashion firms, these factors make it both harder to predict trends and exploit them for profit.

Shift from Style Evolution to Fast Fashion

Until Dior's New Look in 1947, fashion change had been evolutionary, but Dior introduced a new look each season—the H-line, the A-line. People came to expect seasonal newness (Cardin & Charney, 1992). Still, fashion forecasting was relatively simple. The fashion press and merchants focused on a short list of new trends—which were by definition "In"—and the looks appeared in stores after a relatively short time lag. Meanwhile consumers' appetite for the new looks was building through the fashion leadership of women who wore the fashions first and through visibility in the media.

The driver was seasonal change—the expectation among consumers that a change in the season required new clothes with the latest colors, silhouettes, and decorative details. Over time the number of seasons increased from four to six or more. What had been a stately progression from one new look to the next became instead a continuous flow of new trends, each crowding on the heels of the one before. The acceleration of change promoted an appetite for newness among designers, the press, and consumers.

Traditionally, delivering newness took from 9 to 11 months—the product development cycle for sportswear went from sketches to samples to orders to production and delivery to stores. With the help of technology, most companies were able to cut that time line to 5 or 6 months ("The Cycle," 2003). Then, the fast-fashion chains—Spain's Zara and Sweden's Hennes & Mauritz (H&M)—revolutionized fashion retailing by collapsing the time between the runway and the store into days rather than months. The idea was to deliver a large assortment of runway-inspired trends rapidly at a temptingly low price for young trend-hungry consumers. By monitoring sales, these companies can stop production on styles that fail, increase deliveries of hot items, and adjust colors and other aspects in time for the next shipment (Barker, 2002). Forever 21, an American chain, expanded fast fashion from teens to women, men, and children. Using "design merchants" rather than designers (a design process that is proprietary), the company turns out adaptations of runway hits that are almost "indistinguishable from designer clothes" in six weeks (La Ferla, 2007a).

In the late nineteenth century, articles referred to "the style problem," which had three symptoms: rapid change in fashion, the increasing number of styles available each season, and availability of the styles to more people simultaneously (Parsons, 2002). Perhaps today's fast fashion is the tail end of a trend toward making fashion available to consumers at all price ranges.

While fast fashion is clearly ascendant, a countertrend emerged—slow fashion. Like the slow food movement, which seeks to counter a fast-food lifestyle, slow fashion offers respite from constantly chasing trends and fast cycle times. Focusing on "thoughtful beginnings" (a concern for where materials came from and how they were produced), use of well-paid workers, and longer use by consumers, slow

Figure 1.8.
Slow fashion seeks a more eco-conscious, long-term view compared to the disposable approach of fast fashion. Uluru's hand-embellished tunic produced with Alabama Chanin exemplifies the values of the movement. (*WWD*, Courtesy of Fairchild Publications)

fashion can take many forms: classic jeans, couture gowns that hold their value, vintage and classic silhouettes, and neutral colors. A T-shirt made of organic cotton discarded a few months after purchase doesn't qualify as slow fashion. Whether slow fashion catches on or not depends on how the idea is marketed, the ingenuity of designers working within the limitations, and the response from consumers.

Slow fashion may not appeal to fashionistas who are quick to buy and just as quick to discard, but it may appeal to customers looking for clothing that expresses personal style (Tran, 2008c) (Figure 1.8).

What drives fashion today? In the past drivers included newness associated with seasonal change, the desire to wear the latest "In" looks, the wish to be appropriately dressed

Figure 1.9.
When young fashion-forward consumers wanted access to runway trends faster than traditional stores could react, Zara pioneered production and distribution methods that made it possible to satisfy that demand—an example of a co-evolving marketplace.
(Dominique Maitre)

for any occasion, and the desire to impress others with our chic clothes—in a word, to be "cool." Li Edelkoort, head of Trend Union, a Paris-based forecasting agency, expects seasonal and gender boundaries to blur—a prelude to people dressing in more unconventional ways (Gonzalez, 2008). One thing is sure: fashion will always be around. In down times, fashion can be therapeutic. In up times, fashion lets people flaunt their good fortune and enjoy their rewards (Kermouch, 2002). Another sure thing is the co-evolving nature of the marketplace between buyers and sellers (Figure 1.9). The current era has been characterized as postindustrial or postmodern—a label that sounds like the end of something. Perhaps such characterizations are a prelude to change, to a new era with its own new innovations.

FORECASTING IN THE TEXTILE AND APPAREL INDUSTRIES

Even the fastest fast-fashion company needs a picture of what consumers will see as new and exciting. Fashion forecasting provides the tools to create that picture. Whereas fast fashion may meet the needs and interests of some consumers, it cannot cater to all consumer segments, tastes, or price points. Most companies will continue to operate on a longer product-development cycle. Fashion forecasting coordinates the efforts of fiber producers, yarn manufacturers, fabric and print houses, apparel manufacturers, and retailers. As Li Edelkoort, forecaster for Trend Union in Paris, explains, "Trends are meant to have a sense of timing. If you bring them in too early, people just won't get them" (Horton, 2003).

The forecaster stands in the middle of a constantly shifting fashion scene and translates ambiguous and conflicting signals to provide support for business decisions. Although they work with textile fabrications, colors, and styles, their real job is to predict the preferences of consumers in the future. Forecasters work at all stages of the textile/apparel supply chain and on time lines that vary from a few months in advance of the sales season to ten years ahead of it. Each type of forecast and time line has its place in providing decision support for the executive.

Every apparel executive in the fields of product development, merchandising, marketing, and promotion is also a forecaster because those executives make decisions about an uncertain future with incomplete information. In companies today, forecasting must be a team effort, with information shared between design, merchandising, marketing, sales, and promotion, so that the right product gets produced and distributed at the right time to a target consumer. In the world of fashion, improving the success rate of new merchandise, line extensions, and retailing concepts by only a few percentage points more than justifies the investment of time and money in forecasting.

Fashion forecasters share common ground: they believe that by keeping up with the media, analyzing shifts in the culture, interviewing consumers, and dissecting fashion change, they can spot trends before those trends take hold in the marketplace. By anticipating these changes, forecasters allow companies to position their products and fine-tune their marketing to take advantage of new opportunities. Major companies are becoming more and more dependent on this kind of forecasting because traditional forms of purely quantitative forecasting are less applicable to an increasingly volatile and fragmented marketplace.

Short-term forecasting is the process that begins two to three years before the arrival of merchandise in the retail store. This simultaneously collaborative and competitive process allows the segments of the textile/apparel pipeline to coordinate seasonal goods around looks that can be communicated to the customer through the press and stores. The process includes textile development, color forecasting, and style development as showcased in the international fashion shows and manufacturers' showrooms. These sources provide directional information necessary to the timely and successful introduction of seasonal fashion.

The two- to three-year time line of short-term forecasting allows executives to take advantage of developments and position products in the marketplace. However, this time line is not sufficient for decisions related to repositioning or extending product lines, initiating new businesses, reviving brand images, or planning new retail concepts.

FIBER COMPANIES

YARN PRODUCERS

WEAVERS & KNITTERS
Textile Forecasting
6–16 Months Before Finished
Price Goods Inventory

**APPAREL DESIGNERS &
MANUFACTURERS**
Seasonal Forecast
3–8 Months Ahead of
Shipping Date to Retailer

RETAILERS
Order Merchandise
2–6 Months Ahead
of Selling Season

LONG-TERM FORECASTING
Time Horizon More Than
   2 Years Ahead of Selling Season
Economic Cycles
Lifestyle Trends
Social Trends
Consumer Preferences
Trends in the Arts

FIBER/YARN
Structures & Textures

FABRIC
Structures & Textures

FABRIC
Patterns & Prints

COLOR TRENDS
Time Horizon Up to 2 Years
Ahead of Selling Season

DESIGN CONCEPT
Silhouette & Details

STYLE TESTING

SHORT-TERM FORECASTING
Time Horizon Up to 2 Years
Ahead of Selling Season

SALES FORECASTING

Figure 1.10.
Short- and long-term
forecasting operate
on different time lines
depending on whether
they refer to the overall
marketplace or only to
the manufacturing cycle
for apparel.

These decisions require other forecasting approaches with longer time horizons. Long-term forecasting can be more significant for an organization because it looks at social change and demographics. Demographic forecasts are among the most stable types of forecasts. Forecasting social change and technological developments is more difficult (Mahaffie, 1995).

Many people worry that they will not recognize a trend early enough to capitalize on it. Why spend the effort on trendspotting without the expectation of a payoff? Faith Popcorn (1991) says that a shift in lifestyle triggers trend cascades that take about ten years to work through the culture, affect related industries, and reach all market levels. Forecasters working in apparel fields need an early warning system so that trends can be fine-tuned for a specific product category and market segment. Although timing is important, trend information is useful wherever the trend is in its life cycle. Sometimes it is just as important to know when something is on its way out. If a fashion is nearing its termination point, then it is a good time to survey the trendsetters to identify the next big thing. Together, short- and long-term forecasting approaches furnish the textile/apparel executive with access to information and the tools to shape it for decision support.

Forecasting within the Manufacturing Cycle

Short- and long-term forecasting have a more specific time horizon within the **manufacturing cycle** (Figure 1.10). The lynchpin in apparel planning and scheduling is the manufacturer (Michaud, 1989). The forecast is developed by the sales and merchandising managers using input from retailers, marketing representatives, sales history analysis (one to three years of data), and market research. This working, long-term forecast mirrors the manufacturer's business expectations in terms of lines and styles to be produced each month. The short-term forecast includes both basic and fashion goods detailed down to weekly production by style, color, and size. Proper forecasting assures the timely delivery of merchandise to the retailer.

The apparel manufacturer's long-term forecast traces the planning and scheduling process forward to the retailer because it is prepared before orders are received. Orders are shown as input to the short-term forecasts. The quality of the long-term forecast can be measured by comparing expected orders with orders received.

Tracing the planning and scheduling process backward, forecasts and orders feed back to the textile manufacturer. A process very similar to the one in apparel manufacturing occurs at the textile manufacturing level. The time period from initial forecast to delivery of finished piece goods to the apparel manufacturer is between 6 and 16 months. Tracing the process backward one more step leads to the yarn and fiber manufacturers, where a similar forecasting process takes place.

Industry fashion trends enter the model as input for the retailers' decisions and as part of planning at the other stages of apparel, textile, yarn, and fiber manufacturing. Color forecasting is typically done 20 to 24 months ahead of the target selling season. Textile development is typically done 12 to 24 months prior to the target selling season. International fabric fairs show new trends in fabrics one year ahead of the target selling season. All these forecasting activities are aimed at having the right product at the right time to meet customer demand.

Scouting for Fashion Trends

The segments of the fashion industry synthesize information into color and textile forecasts anchored by themes that reflect the spirit of the times. These forecasts serve to coordinate the supply chain for the product development process.

Many organizations and services are available to alert executives to industry fashion trends:

- To-the-trade-only shows showcase fabrics and prints for each season.
- Fashion-reporting services deliver news from the runway and street by subscription on Web sites, through presentations, and in print reports.
- Color forecasters present seminars at industry functions and deliver palettes to members or subscribers.
- Industry trade associations maintain fabric libraries for fashion research and present updates for apparel executives.
- The trade press covers industry events and reports forecasting information.

Members of product development teams, merchandisers, marketers, and retailers participate in events and read the trade press to gather trend information. Some team members are delegated specifically to scout for trend information and locate sources for the latest in fabrics, trims, and findings.

Most apparel companies subscribe to one or more trend services whose job it is to scout the market and report on developments. These services deliver trend information up to two years in advance of the selling season. Sometimes forecasting services are part of a buying office—either an independent organization or a division of a retailing corporation whose role is to scout the market

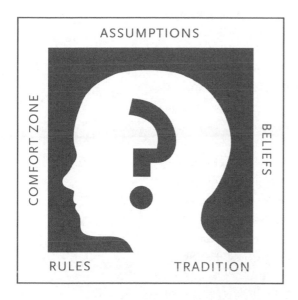

ASSUMPTIONS

COMFORT ZONE

BELIEFS

RULES   TRADITION

THINKING INSIDE THE BOX

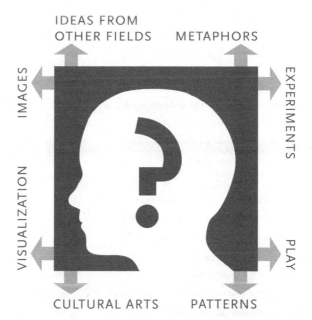

IDEAS FROM
OTHER FIELDS   METAPHORS

IMAGES

VISUALIZATION

EXPERIMENTS

PLAY

CULTURAL ARTS   PATTERNS

THINKING OUTSIDE THE BOX

Figure 1.11.
Solving tame problems requires thinking inside the box. Solving wicked problems means thinking outside the box.

and make merchandise recommendations to stores or chains. Because they serve as coordinating points for trend information, forecasting services exert a considerable influence on the fashion industry (see the Appendix for a listing of these firms).

Forecasting as a Career

The most potent competitive weapon is new ideas (Amabile, 1998). Business creativity has similarities and differences with creativity in the arts. Both kinds of creativity are practiced by people who see potential in new combinations of existing ideas, products, and processes, and by people who persevere during slow periods, especially in the business cycle. But new business ideas must be appropriate and actionable—that is, they must somehow enhance the way business gets done. Creativity in business is based on expertise. Expertise consists of everything a person knows about his or her work domain. The larger the intellectual space that comprises this expertise,

the more chance to discover new possibilities, new connections, and new combinations that solve problems. Working in supportive but diverse teams builds expertise by introducing different perspectives into the dialogue.

Solving problems is the essential element in business: Which new products to introduce? How to put products and likely consumers together in a space conducive to buying? How much to spend on new tools or processes? How to prosper given changing technology and a dynamic marketplace? The first step is to realize the difference between "tame" and "wicked" problems (Pacanowsky, 1995). Tame problems are those that are manageable, easy to define, and lead to a solution that can be applied consistently across time. Wicked problems (a name derived not from the first dictionary meaning of the word, "morally bad," but from another meaning, "harmful and damaging") are so complex that they are very difficult to solve (Figure 1.11).

Because tame problems are manageable, it is relatively easy to gather relevant information and apply traditional methods to discover the solution. The solution to tame problems requires **thinking inside the box** or normal practices. Wicked problems are so difficult that they require **thinking outside the box.** Wicked problems defy easy definition. Forecasting, planning, and strategy development involve wicked problems. The process for solving wicked problems begins by generating the greatest possible understanding of the problem from diverse viewpoints. The trick is to avoid seeking closure too quickly or getting bogged down in a polarizing argument between two positions. Instead, generate a large number of questions that start out:

- "What if . . ." (questions about possibilities)
- "What is . . ." (questions about fact)
- "What should . . ." (questions requiring judgment and opinions)

Sort through the questions and look for those that need to be explored further, and look for relationships and patterns.

Forecasting, with its many disciplines and multiple time horizons, focuses on business creativity. Forecasting professionals are hired by a company for their expertise. Some build on their knowledge of fashion with an insider's view of color, textiles, or styles. Still others are futurists who look at long-term cultural shifts. Some bring the ability to bridge the gap between the corporation and a particular market segment, such as consumers under thirty. As one partner from a research firm that uses young correspondents to track their peers explains:

"A trend is a shift in the prevailing thought process that eventually manifests itself in a range of popular tastes and, ultimately, consumer goods" (McMurdy, 1998). These professional "trend trekkers" work in fashion, but also in related industries such as cosmetics, fragrance, and even cell phones. Lori Smith, a trend forecaster for one of the world's largest makers of perfume, puts it this way: "What I do is bring the outside world in" (Green, 1998). Reports from forecasting professionals—whether working inside the company or as consultants—affect the way a product is designed, the way it is sold, or where it is sold. Salaries are low (mid-$20,000) for entry-level jobs for trend reporters gathering information but forecasters with seven to ten years experience can make in the low six-figures working for a manufacturing, retailing, or established consultancy (Sahadi, 2005). Highly competitive, the field consists of around 1,000 to 1,500 professionals who combine training in fashion, business insight, and a wide-ranging curiosity (Zimmerman, 2008).

One of the best ways to discover if you are a person with the natural gifts and skills required for business creativity is to do an internship with a forecasting company. Consider trade organizations such as Cotton Incorporated, professional organizations such as the Color Association of the United States, retail corporations, buying offices, fashion

● ● ● ACTIVITY 1.4. Surfing for Forecasts
Using a search engine on the Internet, locate Web sites with forecasting information using the keywords "fashion" and "forecast." How often are the sites updated? What organization or company sponsors each site? Bookmark the best sites and check them periodically for updates.

reporting services, and forecasting agencies and consultancies. Check the appendix for a list of possible contacts. Internships are offered on the basis of a company's staffing needs at a particular time. Even if a company has never offered an internship in forecasting, it might offer one to the right applicant at the right time.

To explore your interest in forecasting, create a portfolio. Developing a forecast is only the first step; communicating a forecast is an essential skill. In the portfolio you can demonstrate both these facets. Use the activities in the following chapters as a starting point for the portfolio. Use the portfolio to show your skills in an interview for a forecasting position.

Forecasting professionals are media mavens—sponges for soaking up news that relates to change. Begin your profession by reading the kind of sources that are important to forecasters. By beginning your environmental scanning now, you will build a base for communicating with other forecasters and business executives. A basic media scan would include:

- *The Wall Street Journal* as a substitute for a more extensive scan of business news.
- A national newspaper such as *The New York Times* or another daily from an urban center as a substitute for a more expansive news scan.
- The key trade papers that cover the fashion and apparel industry, including *WWD* (*Women's Wear Daily*) for women's wear and menswear.
- *Advertising Age* for coverage of marketing trends.
- Fashion and lifestyle magazines for coverage of popular culture and opinion leaders that influence fashion trends.

Use an Internet search engine to locate profiles of forecasters. Few if any started as forecasters. Instead, these professionals gained experience in retailing or product development, moving into forecasting as their talents and expertise became valuable enough to support the specialization. By beginning your career with an interest in forecasting, you can choose positions that help deepen and broaden your knowledge of the fashion industry—the kind of background essential to a forecasting professional.

Key Terms and Concepts

Classic

Cohorts

Collective selection

Cycles

Environmental scanning

Fad

Fashion

Fast fashion

Forecasting

Long-term forecasting

Long-wave phenomenon

Manufacturing cycle

Megatrend

Pendulum swing

Planned obsolescence

Point-of-sales (POS) data

Short-term forecasting

Strategic windows

Target market

Thinking inside the box

Thinking outside the box

Trend

Visualization

Zeitgeist

Discussion Questions

The public often considers fashion to be the trivial pursuit of a few people. Instead, fashion is a pervasive process in human culture that plays out in an infinite number of ways. The diversity produces many meanings for words such as fashion, trends, and forecasting. Executives in the apparel industry must be sensitive to the subtle significance of these meanings in order to successfully blend aesthetic concerns with market mindfulness. Use the following questions to summarize and review this chapter.

Defining fashion: What mechanisms in society power fashion behavior? What psychological traits of an individual power fashion behavior? How is meaning transferred in culture?

The spirit of the times: Because it is difficult to recognize the spirit of the times while you are living them, how can forecasters sensitize themselves to cultural patterns? What product category interactions are indicative of the Zeitgeist?

Defining forecasting: What is the role of forecasters inside corporations? What special forecasting disciplines apply to the apparel industry? Is there value to be derived from integrating forecasting disciplines within a company? What kinds of information are useful to forecasters and where do they find that information?

Additional Forecasting Activities

Rules for Appropriateness. What social rules governed fashion in previous decades? Collect oral histories from young adults, people in middle age, and older people. During what time period were they children, teens, and young adults? Ask them to recall things they were taught about appropriate dress. What rules did they have to follow on special occasions, on dates, at school, and at work? When did they notice a relaxation of some of these rules? Should any of these social customs be revived? What would be the effect on the apparel industry?

Cover Stories. Track fashion evolution by looking at the covers of a fashion magazine over the past decade. Libraries often have bound volumes going back decades for the most popular and long-lived magazines. Some magazine Web sites have a section with covers by decade. Because looking at all the covers would take too long, sample the issues by deciding which month or months to examine in each year. Then, systematically look at those covers. Imagine the editor and art director carefully considering the clothes, model, makeup, background color, and all the other elements making up the cover. The cover is the billboard for the magazine and has important implications for newsstand sales. How have cover design and content evolved over the decade? What directional signals for fashion change can you derive from this study? How are fashion magazines changing in the ways they showcase fashion?

Mapping the Zeitgeist. It is difficult to recognize the spirit of the times as you are living through them. To sensitize yourself to this concept, map the Zeitgeist using the categories of dominant events, ideals, social groups, attitude, and technology for the decades from the 1920s to the 1990s. How do these categories define what is remembered about each decade?

Forecasting as a Career Path. Clip articles from trade and popular publications profiling forecasters in all the specialties. Note which work for companies or corporations and which work for consulting firms. Analyze the aspects that are common across all forecasting fields. What courses in your curriculum map to these competencies? Analyze the differences between the forecaster's focus and responsibilities depending on the product category, price point, and target market. What courses in your curriculum encourage the development of specialized knowledge useful in the forecasting process?

Resource Pointers

Business-to-business trend forecasting sites:
StyleSight: www.stylesight.com
WGSN (World Global Style Network): www.wgsn.com
Fashion Snoops: www.fashionsnoops.com
Trendstop: www.trendstop.com
Mudpie: www.mudpie.co.uk

Trend forecasters:
Nelly Rodi: www.nellyrodi.fr/en/index_.html
Peclers Paris: www.peclersparis.com
Li Edelkoort, Trends Union: www.trendsunion.com
PromoStyl: www.promostyl.com

Interior design bloggers:
Cool Hunting: www.coolhunting.com
Apartment Therapy: www.apartmenttherapy.com
Design Sponge: www.designspongeonline.com
MoCo Loco (modern, contemporary):
www.mocoloco.com
UnBeige: www.mediabistro.com/unbeige

PART ONE

FORECASTING
FRAMEWORKS

Trends used to be wonderful because
an idea rippled out, and out, and out,
and eventually, everybody made a
bit of money. Now a trend may have
one or two ripples and die.

—David Wolfe

2
INTRODUCING INNOVATION

OBJECTIVES

- Identify diffusion of innovation as a framework for understanding and predicting fashion change.
- Cultivate skills in analyzing current fashion within a theoretical framework.
- Increase awareness of visualization as a tool of analysis and communication.
- Understand the characteristics of a trend.
- Investigate the diffusion process—how innovations diffuse within a social system, the kind of consumer who participates in each stage, and the social process involved in transmitting fashion innovation.

Diffusion of Innovation

Something new—an **innovation**—is proposed. It may appear in a hit movie, television show, or music video, and influence the buying decisions of millions. Or, it may emerge from the fashion runways as designers return to past fashion eras and spark retro revivals or try to create a modern look with no reference to past fashions. After the innovation arrives on the scene, individuals consider it for adoption. The cumulative effect of those decisions can be tracked in sales and visually on the street.

Sometimes innovation redefines what is appropriate, as in the case of wearing lingerie as outerwear. At first the idea of uncovering bras, lacy teddies, and corsets was totally unacceptable. Then it became daring when rock music divas wore the look in music videos and on stage. Finally the style appeared in modified form in stores everywhere. Eventually echoes of the lingerie look were part of the woman executive's power suit—a lace-edged camisole showing at the neckline of her business suit. Then, fashion moved on and other options became "right" for pairing with business suits. But the lingerie look was extended with the introduction of the slip dress—a style that moved from models on the runway to stores in the mall. The slip dress morphed into layers of transparency with underwear showing, which some retail executives found too daring all over again (Horyn, 2007). The lingerie look continues to be new with each reinvention.

In fashion terms, the innovation may be the invention of a new fiber, a new finish for denim, introduction of an unusual color range, a modification in a silhouette or detail, a different way to wear an accessory, or a mood expressed in a distinctive style (Figure 2.1). When introduced, it diffuses through the population as more and more consumers have a chance either to accept or reject it. This pattern of acceptance or rejection determines the innovation's life cycle. The **diffusion process** maps the response to the innovation over time.

The **diffusion curve**, an idealization of the process, illustrated diffusion of innovation as a bell-shaped curve (Rogers, 1962). The far left side represents early adopters and early diffusion of innovation, the center section, majority adoption, and the right side, laggards

Figure 2.1.
Yves St. Laurent was one of the first to bring innovation from the street onto the runway and his firm continues the tradition with small jackets over volume in the skirts. (*WWD*, Courtesy of Fairchild Publications)

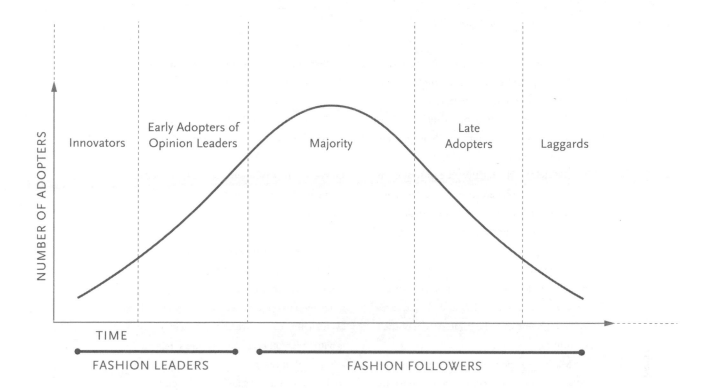

NUMBER OF ADOPTERS

Innovators | Early Adopters of Opinion Leaders | Majority | Late Adopters | Laggards

TIME

FASHION LEADERS   FASHION FOLLOWERS

Figure 2.2.
The diffusion curve is a visualization of the spread of innovation through a social system.

(Figure 2.2). The shape—horizontal time axis and vertical axis for number of adopters—was retained as components of a visualization that came to express many aspects of diffusion.

The most critical stage of the diffusion process comes during the initial introduction. Without **innovators**—people who wear new fashions and expose others to the look—and without **opinion leaders,** who endorse a style to those who seek guidance, no diffusion will take place. For the forecaster, the diffusion model provides a framework for analyzing the movement of an innovation through a social system. The framework helps to answer questions about:

- The innovation—Why do some innovations diffuse more rapidly than others? What characteristics of an innovation help or hinder its adoption?
- The **consumer adoption process**—What is the mental process used by individual consumers in deciding between adopting or failing to adopt an innovation?

- The diffusion process—How do innovations diffuse within a social system? What kind of consumer participates in each stage? What is the social process involved in transmitting fashion innovation?

CHARACTERISTICS OF AN INNOVATION

For something to function as an innovation, the consumer must perceive the newness or novelty of the proposed fashion—it must seem different when compared to what already exists in the wardrobe, across the social group, or in the market environment. This degree of difference from existing forms is the first identifying characteristic of an innovation.

Rogers (1983) identified characteristics that would help or hinder the adoption of an innovation.

- **Relative advantage** is the perception that the innovation is more satisfactory than items that already exist in the same class of products.

- **Compatibility** is an estimate of harmony between the innovation and the values and norms of potential adopters.
- **Complexity** is a gauge of the difficulty faced by a consumer in understanding and using the innovation.
- **Trialability** is the relative ease of testing out the innovation before making a decision.
- **Observability** is the degree of visibility afforded the innovation.

An innovation will be more readily accepted if it is conspicuous, clearly better than other alternatives, easy to understand, simple to try, and congruent with the value system of the consumer.

Marketing and merchandising focus on educating the consumer about an innovation and lowering barriers to its adoption. Spraying consumers with fragrance as they enter a department store increases trialability; ads showing how to wear the latest accessory reduces complexity; the fashion show illustrating how to coordinate new items demonstrates compatibility. Many other marketing tactics are aimed at lowering the barriers to the adoption of a fashion innovation.

One other characteristic inhibits or encourages adoption of innovation—**perceived risk** (Robertson, Zielinski, & Ward, 1984). A consumer, when considering something new and novel, imagines beyond the purchase to the consequences (Venkatraman, 1991). The consequences may involve:

- **Economic risk**—the risk of performance problems after the purchase, that the purchase price may reduce the ability to buy other products, and that the price will fall after purchase.

- **Enjoyment risk**—the risk of becoming bored by the purchase or not liking it as much as expected.
- **Social risk**—the risk that the consumer's social group will not approve.

Lowering the perception of risk is a powerful element in encouraging the adoption of an innovation.

Forecaster's Toolbox: Sizing Up the Innovation

A forecaster uses the characteristics of an innovation to project potential acceptance. First, evaluate the ways in which the new innovation is better than other similar products (relative advantage). If the innovation is clearly superior to the product it will substitute or replace, acceptance is more likely. Then, evaluate the other characteristics for potential barriers to adoption. Can these barriers be reduced or removed through packaging, presentation, providing information, or demonstration? Can the visibility of the innovation be enhanced? What risks may inhibit the consumer's adoption of the innovation? Can the risks be eliminated, reduced, or downplayed? If the barriers to acceptance are low, it is likely that the innovation will enter the process more easily, diffuse more quickly, and be adopted by more consumers.

THE CONSUMER ADOPTION PROCESS

The diffusion curve is a visualization of group dynamics because it captures many individual decisions. In each individual case, a consumer decides to accept or reject a proposed innovation. The consumer's adoption process—the private decision—is performed with consideration of how the adoption will affect the way the consumer

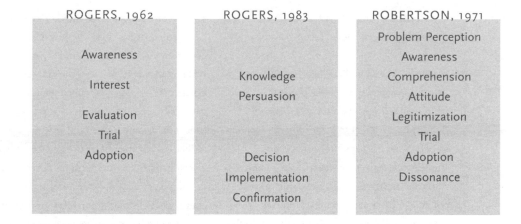

ROGERS, 1962

Awareness

Interest

Evaluation

Trial

Adoption

ROGERS, 1983

Knowledge
Persuasion

Decision
Implementation
Confirmation

ROBERTSON, 1971

Problem Perception
Awareness
Comprehension
Attitude
Legitimization
Trial
Adoption
Dissonance

Figure 2.3.
A comparison of the steps proposed by different researchers for the consumer adoption process.

presents himself or herself to others and how others will react to the result. There are several versions of the steps in this mental process (Figure 2.3). The original formulation of the adoption process by Rogers (1962) included the stages of:

- Awareness—the stage at which a consumer first realizes that an innovation has been proposed.
- Interest—the period when the consumer seeks information about the innovation.
- Evaluation—the time required to evaluate the information and form an attitude toward the innovation.
- Trial—the testing of the innovation before adoption.
- Adoption or rejection of the innovation.

The most recent version of the process as outlined by Rogers (1983) included the following stages:

- Knowledge—a stage similar to awareness at which a consumer first learns of an innovation.
- Persuasion—the period when a consumer forms a favorable or an unfavorable attitude toward the innovation.

- Decision—the activities leading up to adoption or rejection.
- Implementation—actually using the innovation.
- Confirmation—the stage after adoption when a consumer seeks validation that the decision was correct.

Robertson (1971) proposed another model of the adoption process with the following stages:

- Problem perception—the time when a consumer recognizes a need for change.
- Awareness—the stage at which the consumer becomes aware of the innovation.
- Comprehension—the learning period during which the consumer explores the characteristics and function of the innovation.
- Attitude formation—the result of a period of evaluating the innovation.
- **Legitimation**—an optional stage during which the consumer seeks additional information about the innovation.
- Trial—the stage of trying on or experimenting with the innovation.
- Adoption—the ownership stage.
- **Dissonance**—a stage that occurs only when the consumer questions the adoption decision and seeks reassurance.

The Robertson model (1971) is less linear than the original Rogers model (1962) because it recognizes that consumers may skip steps, double back to an earlier stage, or reject the innovation at any point in the process.

The later Rogers version (1983) and the Robertson version both go beyond the adoption stage to what happens afterwards. This after-the-sale stage is crucial in determining consumer satisfaction and increasing the potential for repeat purchases. However, marketers and forecasters frequently ignore this crucial post-purchase evaluation.

Combining the models gives a view of the total process from initiation to purchase to post-purchase assessment. A consumer must first recognize a need—for something new or replacement when a possession reaches the end of its usefulness. In the awareness and interest stage, the consumer finds a possible solution in the marketing environment. By learning about the innovation, trying it, and evaluating it, the consumer forms a positive or negative attitude about the innovation. The consumer decides to buy or not buy the innovation. After purchase the consumer verifies the decision by seeking more information or reassurance from other people. Satisfaction or dissatisfaction with the decision affects the adoption process on future decisions.

One of the most critical stages in the adoption process is the learning phase (Wasson, 1968). If an innovation requires learning of a new habit pattern, that will slow down its adoption. If an innovative product merely replaces an old one and uses the same set of procedures, or even a simplified set, it will gain ready acceptance. An innovation may trigger three kinds of learning: learning a new sequence, learning to perceive new benefits, or learning to perceive the consumer's role in the use of the product. The rare "overnight success" comes when the innovation fills a missing link in a system that has already been adopted. All other innovations must negotiate a learning phase.

For the forecaster, the model points out several opportunities. The process begins when a consumer becomes dissatisfied with the current situation. If a number of consumers feel the same dissatisfaction, astute forecasters may pick up on that feeling and report it as a void in the market—an opportunity to solve the problem with a new product, process, or service.

The forecaster can trace consumer acceptance through the stages of awareness, exploration, and learning to gauge the eventual acceptance rate for the innovation. By monitoring consumers who discontinue the process or reject the innovation at an early stage, the forecaster can suggest ways to package or modify the innovation to overcome barriers to adoption. An early warning about the failure of an innovation

● ● ● activity 2.1. Journal of a Purchase

Keeping a journal is an excellent way to use personal introspection to gain insights on behavior. Ask yourself what is missing from your wardrobe or what possession would satisfy your heart's desire. The market proposes many innovations to answer your need or solve your problem. Keep a journal of the process of evaluating those options. Pay careful attention to your thoughts and feelings at each stage. Did you go through all the steps outlined in Figure 2.3? Which did you skip? At what points did you decide to continue or discontinue shopping? How did you feel at the point of purchase? How did you gauge satisfaction or dissatisfaction after the purchase? What impact will this purchase have on the next?

to capture consumers can prevent losses by curtailing marketing efforts and by preventing overproduction of the item.

Observing the end of the adoption process—the stages after adoption when the consumer evaluates the decision—often reveals a lack of satisfaction. Products rarely deliver the full set of tangible and intangible attributes sought by the consumer. This reality initiates a new cycle with the identification of a problem. The forecaster's function is to recognize the new problem, identify possible solutions, and report to clients on the new opportunity.

FASHION CHANGE AGENTS

Rogers' (1962) original model shows a very small group of innovators who begin the diffusion process followed by a larger group of opinion leaders. Together these consumers are **change agents**, and they perform several important roles in the spread of innovation in their social group:

- They communicate fashion trends visually and verbally.
- They are relatively more knowledgeable and interested in fashion compared to others in their group.
- They have the aesthetic taste and social sensitivity to assemble a stylish look (King & Ring, 1980).

When others recognize them for their abilities, they become **influentials**—group members who establish the standards of dress for others in the group. Change agents are effective because they represent the ideal within the social group.

According to Rogers' (1962) original formulation of the diffusion curve, innovators were expected to make up 2.5 percent of the total adopters; early adopters added an additional 13.5 percent. This model launched innumerable studies of the demographics and psychographics of innovators and opinion leaders, not only in the field of fashion but in all product categories and many kinds of social systems. Behling (1992) reviewed studies that had used Rogers' (1962) diffusion curve as a theoretical framework and where apparel was the product category. She concluded that the research had failed to confirm the subtle gradations of adoption outlined by Rogers. Part of the problem was attributed to the multiplicity of terms used—fashion innovators, fashion leaders, and early adopters—without clearly defining the similarities and differences between these terms. This lack of specificity means that the findings from such studies are interesting and provocative but not as useful as they might have been if the terms had been defined.

One thing is clear, fashion change agents are important to marketers because they control the diffusion of an innovation. A small group of mavens—people with knowledge about some aspect of lifestyle, a passion for newness, and the desire to share their interest with others—produces the **word-of-mouth** to power the spread of an innovation. Journalist Malcolm Gladwell's 2002 book, *The Tipping Point,* explains the influence such people have to spread an idea to a larger audience. As a panel member talking to marketing executives he said, "These people are not necessarily the best educated or wealthiest, but they do have a special social power" ("Marketing," 2003). Edward Keller and Jonathan Berry, in their book *The Influentials,* assert that 10 percent of consumers determine the consumption behavior of the other 90 percent and use findings from 60 years of Roper polls to bolster their claims (2003). Using interpersonal networks, these change agents or influentials act in the early stages of adoption and lay the foundation for later mass acceptance of a trend.

Retailers play a role as change agents in fashion diffusion (Hirschman & Stampfl, 1980). Designers and manufacturers propose many more innovations in a season that can be merchandised in the retail space available. Retailers control the flow of innovation into the social system by selecting among the proposed innovations the ones that will appear in the stores. Some high-fashion stores and avant-garde boutiques are willing to present new fashion innovations based on their own judgment and clientele. They are analogous to the fashion innovators. Other more **mainstream** retailers are like opinion leaders because consumers turn to their assortment, sales associates, and visual merchandising for informed advice and fashion direction.

Innovators

Marketers usually identify innovators as people who buy new product innovations relatively earlier than others in their social group. To target such customers for product introductions, marketers need a profile of such early adopters. The usual profile is of a young, educated, affluent consumer who is very interested in the particular product category. But is there a personality trait that predisposes people to prefer new products? Innovativeness, the desire for new experiences, is such a trait (Hirschman, 1980). Personality traits affect general behaviors more than specific purchases, but they underlie the ways consumers approach, modify, simplify, and react to their marketing environment (Horton, 1979).

Innovative people can be segmented into three groups, each with a different profile (Venkatraman, 1991):

- Cognitive innovators prefer new mental experiences and enjoy novelty when associated with thinking and problem solving.
- Sensory innovators prefer experiences that stimulate the senses, have an easygoing attitude toward life, take risks, participate in pleasurable activities without thinking too much, and engage in dreaming and fantasy.
- Cognitive-sensory innovators prefer both cognitive and sensory experiences.

Fashion apparel has both cognitive and sensory components. Purely stylistic innovations such as a new silhouette, color, or detail make their appeal on sensory grounds (Figure 2.4). Innovativeness in clothing is related to enjoying dressing just for the positive feelings created and for the excitement of experimentation (Pasnak & Ayres, 1969). New fibers and finishes, new ways to wear accessories, and novel coordination strategies are more cognitively appealing as problem solvers.

Although all three types of innovative consumers buy new products and visit new retail stores earlier than other consumers, they vary in other ways. Consumers who prefer new mental experiences monitor more mass media channels, attend more to ads, and do more exploratory shopping such as browsing window displays than other consumers. Sensory innovators prefer visual to verbal information, whereas cognitive innovators are the opposite (Venkatraman & Price, 1990).

Consumers who are first to make fashion purchases and wear new styles often pay a premium price. They are thought to be less price sensitive and more affluent than those who buy later in the season. Researchers found another factor that influences early sales—the degree of confidence the early shopper has in the economic conditions (Allenby, Jen, & Leone, 1996). By comparing sales data from five

Figure 2.4.
Innovators respond
early to the sensory
appeal of new
silhouettes, details,
and style combinations,
and they have the confi-
dence to wear
them ahead of others
in their group.
(*WWD*, Courtesy of
Fairchild Publications)

divisions of retailer, researchers were able to show that consumer confidence about the future state of the economy was a strong predictor of preseason sales. The best predictor for in-season sales was the financial ability to purchase.

Discovering the factors that drive early sales of a fashion item is critical in business planning and forecasting. Early warning about the potential success or failure of a look, line, or stylistic innovation allows managers to adjust pricing and production schedules. (See Chapter 9 for a more extended discussion of consumer confidence and forecasting.)

Fashion Leaders

If innovators are change agents who first adopt a new fashion and make it visible within their social groups, how are fashion leaders described? Katz and Lazarsfeld (1955) sought to answer this question by interviewing women. If the women reported being asked for advice about clothes or believed they were more likely than others to be asked for advice, interviewees were classified as **fashion leaders**.

Katz and Lazarsfeld (1955) identified two kinds of fashion leaders, the glamorous woman who first displays expensive fashions and the woman who is influential face-to-face. When the characteristics of these self-identified fashion leaders were compared to others, the fashion leaders were found to be highly interested in fashion, sensitive to their impression on others, gregarious, and recognized as having qualities appropriate for leadership. The researchers found that single, unmarried women with a high interest in fashion had more opportunities for fashion leadership than women at other points in the life cycle. Unexpectedly, findings showed very little difference in the incidence of fashion leaders in different social classes. However, women in the lower class were more

likely to seek leadership outside their class. Influence takes place mostly among women of similar circumstances and real-life groups—that is, in naturally occurring groups of friends, colleagues, neighbors, and acquaintances.

Almost 20 years later and with young, single women, Schrank (1973) confirmed the earlier findings about fashion leadership. She administered a fashion leadership scale and a clothing interest inventory to college women and interviewed them about 15 clothing or accessory items with varying degrees of diffusion. Respondents indicated which of the items they owned and when they had been purchased. Schrank found there was a significant relationship between fashion leadership and clothing interest and that fashion leadership is evenly distributed through all social classes.

If people have similar attitudes toward fashion, the difference between leaders and followers is a matter of intensity and speed of adaptation (Brenninkmeyer, 1973). In this view, fashion leaders are more susceptible to change and more interested in differentiating themselves from others. In terms of self-concept, fashion leaders consider themselves more excitable, indulgent, contemporary, formal, colorful, and vain than followers (Goldsmith, Flynn, & Moore, 1996). A fashion leader must be talented enough to sense the spirit of the times and anticipate change in tastes, self-confident enough to make her own fashion choices, and influential within her social group.

Leaders also differ from followers in terms of information seeking. Leaders and followers all use the same sources of fashion information, but leaders use a greater number of sources more frequently and more often preferred marketer-dominated sources—window and in-store displays, fashion magazines, and fashion shows (Polegato & Wall, 1980).

Celebrities as Innovators and Influentials

Popular culture includes advertising, movies, television, music, magazines, and celebrity news. Popular culture serves as a source of new meanings and as a conduit to transmit those meanings to people (McCracken, 1988b). Slang expressions, lifestyles, sports and pastimes, personality and mood—popular culture is a visual dictionary of meanings. Mass media constantly revise the meanings of old goods and give meaning to new goods. In this way popular culture acts as innovator and as a **distant opinion leader** for consumer culture.

The connection between celebrities and products is not new. It began in the 1860s when Adah Isaacs Menken, a popular New York stage star, allowed Madame Marguerite to advertise that she was dressmaker for the star. Menken was compensated with a new wardrobe. Fifteen years later, Dr. Gouraud, a purveyor of cosmetics, not satisfied to simply link his products with the beauty of the Queen of Sheba and the wisdom of Solomon, pioneered celebrity endorsement with advertisements that featured testimonials from actresses and singers popular at the time (Banner, 1983). In 1927, the Thompson advertising agency launched a campaign in which Hollywood stars praised the skin-care qualities of Lux soap (Fox, 1984). The practice of star endorsement was well established by the early 1940s.

●●● activity 2.2. Fashion Measures

Researchers have developed questionnaires that measure fashion leadership, fashion interest, and innovativeness. Take the measures yourself. What does your score indicate about you? Have others in your class take the measures but do not attach any names or numbers that identify individuals. Score the measures and report on the findings. What do the scores reveal? Measures such as these are the building blocks for consumer research on consumer behavior and fashion leadership.

The question of celebrity credibility was already a topic of concern in the 1920s. Starlet Constance Talmadge appeared as an endorser in eight ads for eight different products in a single national magazine in 1927—an early case of celebrity overexposure. By the 1950s, the public's attitude toward celebrity advertising had changed from one in which a celebrity could sell just about anything to a rejection of testimonials as insincere (Fox, 1984).

If consumers are suspicious of the motives of celebrity endorsers, how effective can they be? Advertising practitioners rely on a celebrity face to cut through the clutter of ad messages with the shock of recognition and expect the likeability of the celebrity to transfer to the product. If consumers are skeptical of celebrity endorsements, how can celebrities function as opinion leaders? The relationship between viewer and celebrity is as psychologically complex as any other relationship.

Media performers create the illusion of interpersonal relationships with viewers. In today's media-rich environment, relationships of this imaginary sort are intertwined with media experiences (Horton & Wohl, 1956). The real social world consists of a few hundred relatives, friends, and acquaintances a person actually knows. The artificial social world consists of celebrities and the characters they play. Although the relationship takes place in the imagination, people identify with celebrities and feel as if they know them (Caughey, 1978). Social behavior and consumer purchasing can be influenced by media personalities because they act as advisors, role models, and ego ideals (Figure 2.5).

For fashion, movies have been a great medium for showing clothes. A big-screen image can be influential for decades—Marlon Brando in a white T-shirt from *The Wild Ones*, Joan Crawford's padded shoulders and tailored suits in the 1940s, John Travolta's wardrobe in *Saturday Night Fever* and *Urban Cowboy*, Jennifer Beals in a torn sweatshirt in *Flashdance*. More recently movies as different as the *Pirates of the Caribbean* series with its look of romantic dishabille and the *Oceans* series showing off slick Las Vegas styles inspired consumers and retailers. Hollywood designers followed trends and set them. The actors, as well as the characters they play, act as influentials in their lifestyle choices and public appearances. A magazine editor explained that the red carpet at an awards show "is a runway show for us. The pickup pictures are the most important thing. Put [a star in a designer's dress] and the pictures turn up over and over again. Designers love the exposure. It's the equivalent of $10 million in free advertising" (La Ferla, 2003). Music stars showcased in music videos have been influential in setting and popularizing trends. From *Miami Vice* to *Mad Men*, every year or so clothing styles worn by characters in television shows excite demand for the same clothes in stores. Findings from a survey of 2,500 women (sponsored by a firm that covers celebrities) found that consumers look beyond the A-list to up-and-coming stars for fashion inspiration and beyond the red carpet to candid photos of the stars in real-life situations where styles are more accessible ("Celebrity," 2008).

The consumption of fashion goods and intangible products such as fragrance is more involved than mere purchase behavior. Consumption is a cultural phenomenon and the designers, advertising executives, and fashion press participate in creating our cultural universe by connecting meaning to consumer goods. Consumers construct their personal worlds by choosing the products that have meaning for them (McCracken, 1988b). In this process, pop culture has both direct and indirect influence on the consumer's ideas about appropriateness, beauty, and fashion.

Fashion Followers

Fashion followers include both the majority adopters who swell the diffusion curve to its highest point as well as those who adopt after that. After the peak, the number of new adopters decreases until all people who are interested in the innovation have had the opportunity to possess it or at least try it.

If the innovation is a major trend affecting a large number of consumers over several seasons or even several years, manufacturers and retailers still have an opportunity for profit at the peak of adoption and as the innovation reaches the late adopters. If the trend is a short-lived fad, the time scale is much shorter and the potential for profit is better for manufacturers and retailers participating in the early stages. For the forecaster, the waning of a trend signals the potential for adoption of a new innovation, one that probably already exists and is beginning its diffusion cycle.

● ● ● activity 2.3. Star Map

Celebrities appeal to different groups of consumers. What movies, television shows, actors, bands, and singers are influential with the demographic group identified as "young adults"? Is there a difference between celebrities who are influential with fashion innovators, and those who influence fashion leaders and fashion followers? Map the celebrities most influential for each group and present your findings as a portfolio spread or as a PowerPoint presentation.

Figure 2.5.
Celebrities function as advisors, role models, and represent the ideal image for consumers. Some celebrities are multitasking as fashion consumers and designers—Victoria Beckham and Jennifer Lopez in the front row for a Marc Jacobs show. (*WWD*, Courtesy of Fairchild Publications)

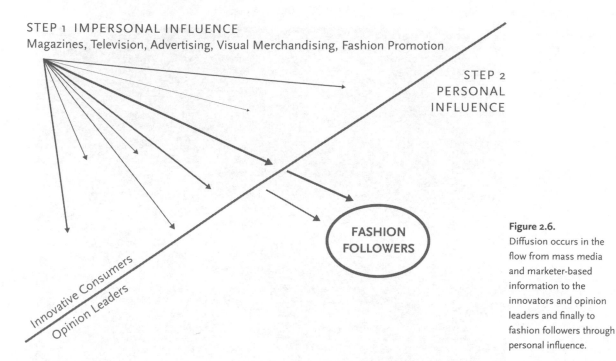

STEP 1 IMPERSONAL INFLUENCE
Magazines, Television, Advertising, Visual Merchandising, Fashion Promotion

STEP 2 PERSONAL INFLUENCE

Innovative Consumers
Opinion Leaders

FASHION FOLLOWERS

Figure 2.6.
Diffusion occurs in the flow from mass media and marketer-based information to the innovators and opinion leaders and finally to fashion followers through personal influence.

FORECASTER'S TOOLBOX: VISUALIZING THE DIFFUSION PROCESS

The visualization of diffusion in the Rogers model (1962) shows a **two-step flow** (Figure 2.6). The first step involves transmission of new ideas through the impersonal influence of mass media and marketer-based information to innovators and opinion leaders. The second step depends on the personal, face-to-face influence within social groups as new ideas move from fashion leaders to fashion followers.

An alternative diffusion model—the Bass model (1969)—makes this point even more explicitly. Instead of defining adopters only by the time period, the Bass model differentiates between the kinds of influence that most contribute to the decision. The visualization of the Bass model shows that most consumers at the beginning of the diffusion process adopt the innovation based on impersonal influences such as the mass media (Figure 2.7). Most subsequent adopters make the

decision based on interpersonal influence. But some adopters, even at the later stages, rely mostly on external, impersonal influence.

The bell curve of the Rogers diffusion process can be redrafted into a cumulative form—the **S-curve**—which more clearly mirrors the growth phase of the product cycle (Brown, 1992). Using this visualization, it is easy to see how an innovation could spread between social groups and market segments (Figure 2.8). For example, a series of S-curves could represent the spread of an innovation from a younger, hip, edgy consumer segment to one that is more educated and affluent, and then to one that is older and more mainstream. Or, the series of S-curves could represent the transmission of the innovation from one company to another, each targeting a different consumer segment. At the first stage, when an innovative product is introduced, a company targeting early adopters sells it. If successful with that first audience, the innovation is picked up by a second company targeting the next group

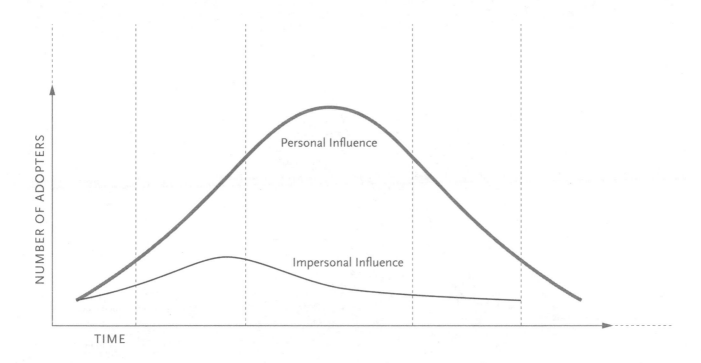

Figure 2.7. (*above*)
The Bass model, an alternative diffusion model, shows that external, impersonal, and marketer-based influences are involved in the rate of adoption through the entire process rather than exclusively at the beginning, as in the Rogers model.

Figure 2.8. (*below*)
In the cumulative form, the bell curve becomes the S-curve. S-curves can be linked to visualize filling market niches segment by segment.

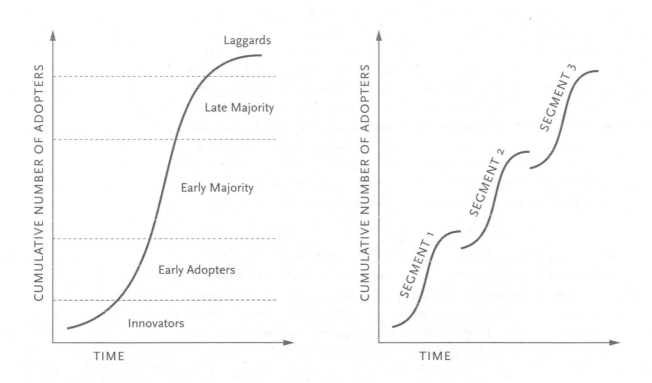

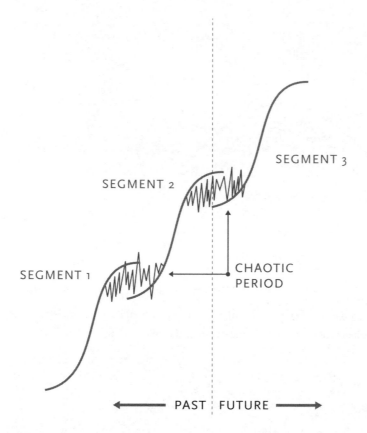

SEGMENT 3

SEGMENT 2

SEGMENT 1

CHAOTIC
PERIOD

←—— PAST | FUTURE ——→

Figure 2.9.
As an innovation moves
from one market niche
to another, the period
of instability during the
change can be visualized
as a period of chaos be-
tween periods of stable
growth.

of adopters, and finally by a third company targeting the volume market. Visualization using the S-curve provides a complex understanding of the diffusion of innovation and a finer-grained framework for forecasting.

Modis (1992) suggests an even more intriguing elaboration on diffusion of innovation. He argues that the S-curve can be used to describe all forms of market growth. He then links a series of curves as Brown did. Finally, using data from a number of industries, he introduces the idea of chaos at the point where the curves overlap (Figure 2.9). In this visualization, the innovation is introduced and

goes through the growth cycle until that market niche is filled; then begins a period of chaos during which a new niche is identified. When identified, another growth cycle begins, and so on.

The bell curve describes the process of diffusion within a social system. Its cumulative form, the S-curve, linked in sequence, shows the process of diffusion as it spreads from one social system or market segment to the next. Failure to fill a niche in this progression signals the end of the innovation's life cycle. Success in filling the next niche indicates the potential for continued diffusion of the innovation to a wider

● ● ● activity 2.4. S-Curves Past, Present, and Future

Backcast an innovation using the linked diffusion curves as a visualization tool. Select a style or fashion item that is at a midpoint in its potential diffusion, perhaps a style that is currently being featured in fashion magazines. Trace it back to its origins. What was the first market niche it reached? Plot the time line as it filled that niche. What was the next market niche? Continue until you bring the style or fashion item to its current market position. Using the S-curves, forecast its next market segment and the timing to fill that niche.

audience. For the forecaster, this visualization holds out the tantalizing idea that such patterns of niche filling could be identified in sales data and be used to predict future patterns.

The chaotic phase between S-curves can be seen as a period during which the innovators in another social system experiment with the innovation. If these innovators adopt the innovation, it is passed to the opinion leaders and continues until that niche is filled.

The idea of a chaotic phase between growth cycles is intriguing. It raises the possibility that a chaotic phase is a precursor to a more stable and predictable growth curve. It is during a chaotic phase that the forecaster's job becomes important to a company. By evaluating the innovation's characteristics, possible barriers to consumer adoption, the influence of change agents, and any self-limiting factors, the forecaster helps a company anticipate the future spread of the innovation to other consumer groups and other markets.

Visualization provides the forecaster with a way to structure observations, determine potential markets for the innovation, and estimate the timing when the innovation will reach new consumer segments. Analysis of diffusion in terms of the curves allows the forecaster to take a snapshot of the current situation, **backcast** to explain the past events, and forecast future developments.

Monitoring Change Agents

By monitoring the acceptance of a given style by change agents, the forecaster has a window on the innovation's level of visibility and the likelihood it will be widely accepted. But change agents are not a stable segment that can easily be targeted. A change agent may be influential regarding the performance of one role, in one product category such as activewear, or only at certain times, and a follower on other occasions (King & Ring, 1980).

Innovator types interact with the characteristics of the innovation—relative advantage, compatibility, complexity, trialability, observability, and risk—to determine marketing strategies (Venkatraman, 1991). Relative advantage will be important to all consumers considering a new product but different innovator types will vary in other preferences.

- Strategy for cognitive innovators— Cognitive innovators are problem solvers who can figure out product complexity and analyze economic risk, but they are not risk takers. Because they closely monitor mass media and pay attention to advertising, the most effective strategy is to present ads that emphasize the relative advantage, provide the information for assessing economic risk, and reduce concerns about enjoyment risk.
- Strategy for sensory innovators—For sensory innovators, the most effective strategy is to reduce complexity and perception of risk while emphasizing the uniqueness of the product and the pleasures associated with it as a visual presentation.

By positioning new fashion innovations as congruent with the fashion leader's self-concept, designers, manufacturers, retailers, and marketers can attract the attention of these important consumers. Although they may not be the very first to adopt the innovation, leaders are early adopters who are very influential within their social groups. Followers do not monitor marketer-dominated information sources to the same degree as innovators and fashion leaders do. For the fashion follower, personal influence from a leader within the social group is much more compelling as an incentive to change.

Figure 2.10.
Topshop in London is a
popular trendspotting
location for fashion-
forward consumers,
stylists, designers,
and forecasters.
(*WWD,* Courtesy of
Fairchild Publications)

Similar to individuals, social groups can act as fashion leaders. If a social group has a high proportion of leaders and frequent interaction with other groups, that group is more likely to export leadership to the other groups. Membership in one group may overlap another, allowing some individuals to serve as links between two or more cliques (Rogers, 1983). Understanding this between-group exchange suggests that adoption of an innovation will be enhanced if marketers target influential social groups and individuals who act as liaisons between groups.

The transfer of meaning from the cultural universe to the construction of an individual's lifestyle has implications for forecasting. Celebrities function as advisors, role models, and ego ideals on two levels—as themselves in interviews and editorial coverage, and as the fictional roles they play. For innovations in which celebrity leadership is a factor, the forecaster can map celebrity influence to the consumer segment most likely to be influenced. The visibility and desirability of the celebrity image may be a determining factor in the diffusion of some innovations.

The Forecaster's Observation Post

The idea that fashion leaders—influential individuals, social groups, celebrities, and retailers—adopt an innovation and transmit it to others provides the forecaster with an observation target. The forecaster can monitor the second stage of the diffusion process by monitoring fashion leaders. The forecaster may choose to watch for fashion leadership in particular geographic markets where innovations are most likely to be introduced and then predict the potential diffusion to other locales with an estimate of the timing (Figure 2.10). Or, a forecaster may watch for fashion leadership in a particular market segment and predict the potential diffusion of an innovation within that segment and as a crossover innovation for other segments. Or, a forecaster may monitor the retailers who perform as change agents and estimate the path of an innovation from avant-garde retailers to more mainstream or mass-market clients. Or, watch celebrities and the looks and behaviors they are likely to popularize with a particular audience.

Trends even affect the profession of "trendspotting." In the late 1990s, "cool hunting" was a popular approach to identifying the next new thing. Cool kids were sent out to interview and photograph other cool kids. The idea was to watch the edgiest, most fashion-forward young people as an early warning system for developing trends. The problem was that trends identified in this way failed to generate much business. Trendspotters learned that the most leading-edge person was too advanced to lead mainstream fashion. It was more important to track the most popular people—teens, celebrities, designers—rather than the edgiest ones because trends must click with the mainstream to generate high-volume sales (Seckler, 2002). The goal of such studies was to pinpoint the prime drivers that guide people's consumption decisions.

Fashion Trends

An innovative look appears in the street, on the runway, or in the media thanks to a trendsetter's ability to go ahead of current fashion, ignoring trends and yet anticipating them (Furchgott, 1998). The look has the appeal of "newness" because it has been missing or scarce in the marketplace. A trend is characterized by a building awareness of this new look and an accelerating demand among consumers (Perna,

1987). A study of fashion change shows that new looks rarely come out of the blue. Instead, fashion is a logical evolution from a precursor, the next step in building on a successful trial balloon, a response to social change, or an expression of cultural drift.

EVOLUTION OF A TREND

Tracking trends is very much like watching weather patterns. A warm and a cool air mass collide, and the result may be a tornado and golf-ball-size hail or just rain and gusty winds. Lawrence Samuel, cofounder of the marketing consulting firm Iconoculture, Inc., spelled out the predictable and unpredictable stages in the **evolution of a trend** ("Will cigars," 1997). The three stages are:

- Fringe—a stage when an innovation arises and the trendiest consumers and entrepreneurial firms begin to participate.
- Trendy—a stage when awareness of the trend grows because early adopters join the innovators to increase the visibility of the trend and the most fashion-forward brands and retailers test the concept.
- Mainstream—a stage when more conservative consumers join in, visibility continues to increase, and corporations and brands capitalize on the growing demand.

Surfing, skateboarding, and snowboarding all started at the fringe of the sports world among a small group of enthusiasts. Each group evolved an identifying style and entrepreneurial firms sprang up to supply the look. When more people became aware of the sports, as participants or fans, the styles became trendy. Fashion journalists and forecasters began to identify the style as fashion forward and some large brands began to test the looks in small collections in wide distribution. Top surf, skate,

● ● ● activity 2.5. Small Changes

Trace the evolution of the men's suit in the twentieth century. Working within a narrow band of allowable fashion change, men's suits have still displayed the influence of fashion trends on silhouette, fabric, and details. Use primary sources—publications from the time when the clothing was new. Collect examples including photographs of celebrities, newspaper ads, and offerings in mail-order catalogs. Identify the aspects of the suit that vary across time. How much variation is there between extremes? Do any aspects vary together as a recognizable pattern? Observing the details in the evolution of men's suits helps sensitize the eye to subtle variations in styles.

and snowboarding brands expanded their range into more classic looks as the sports gained recognition and acceptance. As one executive explained, "skateboarding sport has become so large and has such a following that anyone can find their style" (Weisman, 2008).

The sports and characteristic styles moved from fringe to trendy to mainstream but with some interesting variations. Urban influences like hip-hop became directional for surf, skate, and snowboarding apparel and accessories—a fusing of two trends. Graphic T-shirts and hooded sweatshirts (known as "hoodies"), key items for skaters, were easily assimilated into mainstream fashion. But more extreme styles like pipe jeans remained niche products. The pendulum of style swung from punk-rock styles with prominent logos in the 1990s to more conservative looks with classic polo shirts and V-neck sweaters with discreet logos in the mid-2000s. During trend evolution one of several things might happen. At any stage, a trend can meet resistance, merge with another trend, be deflected in a way that changes the course of the trend, or fragment into microtrends. The microtrends may be countercultural twists on the trend, a reinvention, a countertrend (the opposite of the original trend), or a backlash— all create a new trend back at the fringe stage.

Fashions, Fads, and Classics

The terms *fad* and *classic* are frequently used in discussing fashion, but do they have a precise meaning? Fads have been defined in different ways:

- As involving fewer people, of shorter duration, and more personal than other fashion changes (Sapir, 1931).
- As outside historical continuity—each springing up independently with no forerunner and no successor (Blumer, 1969).
- As satisfying only one main need, the need for a new experience, and having little value after the newness wears off (Wasson, 1968).

Fashions are themselves of short duration when compared to long-term social changes. Fads are fashions of even shorter duration. The difference between fads, fashions, and classics can be visualized using variations on the diffusion curve (see Figure 1.2 in the previous chapter). Classics are enduring styles that seem to reach a plateau of acceptance that endures for a long period of time.

Fashion and fads share many of the same characteristics. Meyersohn and Katz (1957) offer a comprehensive natural history of fads identifying these distinctive characteristics:

- Fads are typically confined to particular segments in society.
- Unlike new social movements that create a new social structure, fads move swiftly through a subgroup but leave the subgroup itself stable.
- Fads offer a simple substitution for some predecessor item.
- Fads are trivial, not in terms of the emotion or functional significance of the item, but in terms of its life expectancy—a fad is susceptible to being outmoded.

Meyersohn and Katz (1957) assert that fads are not born but rediscovered from a style that existed all along in the lives of some subgroup. Likely beginning points for fads include the upper classes and bohemians because these groups represent a special kind of laboratory where experimentation can take place without threatening society as a whole. Many other observers of fashion recognize the same source for fashion ideas—the elite and the outsiders.

Innovative ideas are discovered by fashion scouts and moved from source to marketplace by **tastemakers**. Scouts—journalists, fashion directors, forecasters, and merchants—have the ability to recognize and transmit fads from the subgroup to the mainstream because they have a unique understanding of both. Tastemakers—celebrities, models, fashion stylists, and fashion leaders—increase the visibility of the innovation and make it acceptable to more consumers. Exporting a fad to a wider audience usually involves modifying the idea in ways that make it more acceptable to a broader audience.

The classic is a style that changes minimally over time. It remains within the acceptable range in terms of attributes offered and expenditure in terms of time and money. Classics represent midpoint compromises that deliver at least the core attributes desirable to the consumer (Wasson, 1968). Additionally, classics appeal to a special kind of personality seeking to avoid extremes in styling.

Forecasters seeking to visualize the way trends move through culture have several alternatives. The movement can be seen as:

- An information cascade from fashion leaders to followers.
- Attachment of a catchy label (important to a trend's popularity), a coattail effect during

which the trend builds among the most fashion forward, and flow where it moves into the mainstream.

- Trickling down from the elite, up from the street, and across consumer segments.
- Contagion where the trend moves from person to person like the flu.

Each alternative adds to forecasters' ability to spot and track trends.

Information Cascades

Rarely do consumers make decisions in a situation in which all relevant information is available. Imitating a fashion leader is a strategy frequently used in uncertain situations. Fashion followers presume that the fashion leader has more accurate and precise information (Bikchandani, Hirshleifer, & Welch, 1992).

When an innovation is introduced and a fashion leader acts to adopt or reject the innovation, frequently others imitate the action, beginning an **information cascade** of decisions. Information cascades can be positive, when all individuals adopt the innovation, or negative, when all individuals reject the innovation. If these important leaders do in fact have more accurate and precise information and make a good decision initially, then the information cascade will continue. However, if that initial decision was faulty, the information cascade will be fragile and prone to fall apart. Additional information or a slight value change can shatter a cascade.

The idea of cascade reactions reinforces the disproportionate effect a few early individuals may have on the life span of an innovation. These cascade reactions explain fads, booms, and crashes, as well as other short-lived fluctuations that appear to be whimsical and without obvious external stimulus.

Label, Coattail, and Flow

Of the many ideas on the runway, only a few are successful in attracting backing. In the first 100 years of modern fashion, this backing came from clients. Some fashion counts from that period show that only one-tenth of the designs were produced for clients (Lipovetsky, 1994). The rest were neglected, forgotten, and replaced by a new crop of proposed fashion ideas in the next season. The **gatekeeper** role initially played by clients was taken over by merchants and by the fashion press. The merchants decide which fashion ideas will be available to consumers, which will be made in small numbers, and which in volume. The fashion press defines trends by deciding which of the many ideas on the runway will be promoted in the pages of trade publications and fashion magazines.

In the past, collections could be categorized as either "editorial" (providing a hook for telling a story or creating a fantasy) or "retail" (wearable, targeted for a consumer segment). Now the press and the merchants tend to be in sync on the looks that will be tested further in the marketplace (Socha, 1998b). Editors know that readers buy from the pages of the magazine and that everything shown must be available at retail. Both magazines and stores cover established designers and new talents. More than ever, editors and store executives share information—key fashion stores invite editors to see what they are buying and creating in private label merchandise for a season; store fashion directors carefully analyze the press's approach. Designers have to be realistic about appealing to both the needs of retailers and the press.

Trends once identified must be given a name, label, or slogan that can be used as a popular identifier (Meyersohn & Katz, 1957). If the name is synchronous with the spirit of the times, original, and catchy, it will speed

●●● activity 2.6. Naming Names

Labeling an innovation can mean the difference between rapid diffusion and failure to adopt the innovation. Forecasters are often part of the process of giving an innovation a label. A catchy name or slogan becomes part of the language and increases the visibility and desirability of a fashion product. Begin with the term "bikini" as an identifier for a two-piece swimsuit or "little black dress" for a simple, unadorned, basic black sheath. Look back in fashion history and research some of the fashion labels we take for granted. How did they originate? What effect did they have on the rate of acceptance? What labels are being applied to today's fashion innovations?

the trend on its way. With the **labeling** comes a surge in interest. This surge of interest catches the attention of people in the industry who recognize the potential of the trend and rush to produce it in their own lines. This phenomenon is called the **coattail effect** (or the bandwagon effect). Popular at first with a relatively small sphere of fashionistas, the trend will pass from group to group across social boundaries of age, income, and lifestyle—a process called **flow.**

Dior did not call his post–World War II rediscovery of close-fitting bodices, small waists, and full skirts "the New Look." A journalist used that term in a review of the designer's collection. The term stuck because it captured the spirit of that time, the radical change in silhouette that resonated with change in all aspects of life. With the labeling comes a surge in interest. Then a coattail effect begins when industry people recognize the potential of the fad and produce it and other related products. Flow results when the fad passes from group to group across social boundary lines. If the innovation has broad appeal and staying power, the fad transforms into a fashion. With "the New Look" this process took less than one year.

Jumping on the bandwagon (or catching the coattail) of a fad is tricky, but there are some guidelines for this maneuver (Reynold,

1968). Greater staying power is achieved if the innovation meets a genuine need or function, is associated with other long-term trends and concurrent trends in other industries, is compatible with the values of society, and has high visibility. The problem for designers in assessing a fad is that they may see trends where none exist—that is, their point of view tends to exaggerate the importance of fads. The problem for managers is that they may delay to the point where they miss an opportunity to participate.

Purchase decisions are the result of an approach-avoidance reaction. When the buyer sees potential satisfaction of a need, want, or aspiration in the possession of a good, then the buyer makes the purchase. If the satisfaction sought is thwarted by price, by the effort of searching, or by some compromise in product design, the purchase will not be made. Every purchase is a compromise between the attributes desired and the product that is offered.

Up, Down, Across

Tracking trend movement may require only a few points to plot a line and detect a direction. The trend may be moving up from the street through levels of consumers from the most avant-garde to the more mainstream or down from an extravagant one-of-a-kind couture creation worn by a celebrity to a knockoff at the local mall. Horizontal movement occurs when more and more people progressively adopt a style as that innovation diffuses through the market segments.

The cyclical nature of fashion can be seen in the recycling of fashion ideas—such as the popularity of early-1960s dress styles in the late 2000s. Fueled partly by nostalgia among generations old enough to remember and partly by the younger generation's desire to experience the music and fashions of another era, pop culture seems to circle back, picking up speed each time (Wolcott, 1998). Looking for these movements, placing observations within a theoretical framework, and visualizing the shape and direction of the change enables forecasters to predict fashion direction and the speed of change.

Contagion

The transmission of trends has been likened to the spread of a virus. Malcolm Gladwell, a writer for *The New Yorker*, used this metaphor when he spoke to the International Design Conference about creating design trends that are "contagious"—spreading quickly through the consumer population to reach "epidemic" proportions. He urged manufacturers to aim for "sticky" looks with flulike staying power because consumers do not want looks that quickly disappear (Feitelberg, 1998a). Authors Chip and Dan Heath (2007) extend Gladwell's ideas by identifying the key principles for turning ordinary ideas into those with "stickiness": simplicity, unexpectedness, concreteness, credibility, emotionally involving, and easily communicated through stories.

Gladwell's comments parallel the concept of **memes**—self-replicating ideas or bits of behavior that move through time and space without continuing support from their original source (Gelb, 1997; Kauffman, 1995). Memes can be advertising slogans, catchy bits of dialogue from a television show, or any concept that establishes its own repetition by appearing in many formats. The more copies of the meme, the more likely that it will replicate through time and space. A product, a look, or a brand can become a meme. The characteristics of a meme are very similar to a trend: novelty and vividness. A meme has one additional important characteristic: it must catch on in a way that

favors the leaping of the meme from format to format at a rapid speed.

Trends must be visible to possible adopters in order to spread. Trends spread through word-of-mouth among personal networks when one person visually or verbally recommends a new fashion to friends and acquaintances (Figure 2.11). **Buzz**—defined as excitement about something new—is created when trends pass through media networks, moving from one format to another (from news magazines to talk shows, from the morning shows to late-night). Receiving information on a trend in this way gives the consumer a feeling of being "in the know" because of insider information from the media elite (Marin & Van Boven, 1998). Buzz lifts whatever people in the media are currently talking about to a new level of awareness. The Internet speeds up the transmission of buzz by preempting traditional media—that is, by breaking news about celebrities, new products, new shopping venues, upcoming movies, and other such happenings before the items can appear in traditional channels (newspapers, magazines, television, radio, and movies). As consumers rely more and more on nontraditional channels for information, **hype**—the artificially generated PR form of buzz—becomes less influential and buzz more influential for trendsetters and early adopters. Public relations (PR) executives know this and try to create buzz by planting information in "under the radar" kinds of campaigns—that is, campaigns disguised as consumer-to-consumer exchanges such as those at social networking and blog sites.

Viral marketing (also called guerrilla marketing) builds on the power of word-of-mouth in personal networks and buzz in media networks. The idea is to spread a message to a wide population by beginning with a few key carriers.

Figure 2.11.
Trends are contagious and spread through social networks of friends and acquaintances. (*WWD*, Courtesy of Fairchild Publications)

Because many people have grown up with traditional marketing, they may become resistant to its ploys. Viral marketing gives them the feeling that they are discovering products through personal or media networks in a way that makes them "in the know" when compared to the rest of society. Practitioners of viral marketing may:

- Field "street teams" of young people who visit clubs, sporting events, concerts, and other hot spots in urban markets and distribute stickers, posters, or other promotional freebies to encourage word-of-mouth on a product or brand (Knight, 1999).
- Create an event such as an unfolding drama acted out on adjacent billboards placed in a prime urban location (Lloyd, 2007).
- Give away next season's designs to editors, stylists, artists, deejays, Internet entrepreneurs, writers, and other cultural creatives who may be seen and photographed wearing the designs as a way to build buzz—a process called product seeding (Socha & Ozzard, 2000).

Whatever its form, viral marketing usually includes something free, cross-linking influences (e.g., fashion and music, art, or sports), piggybacking on other events, using multiple channels (e.g., an event plus a Web site and media coverage), and meshing promotion with natural occurring behaviors (e.g., street teams and stencil campaigns).

Trends End

How can forecasters anticipate the life expectancy of fads? Look at the self-limiting factors because they are more predictive than merely visual or aesthetic considerations (Reynold, 1968). Take low-rise jeans—how low could they go? Five-inch rise for the young, toned consumer was moderated to eight-inch rise for more mainstream consumers. Contoured waistbands to reduce the exposure of derrière extended the look to a broader audience (Malone, 2002). Stylistic, technological, or functional modifications can lengthen the life of the fad.

Paul Poiret, a great couturier of the early twentieth century and master of fashion change, said that "all fashions end in excess"—that is, a fashion can never retreat gradually in good order but instead collapses (Robinson, 1958). Look at the craze for embellishment that recurs every few years. The idea of lace appliqué or embroidery or beading begins as a bit of novelty and ends being a head-to-toe feature. At that point, the trend collapses in favor of less decorated or even minimal looks.

To make the jump from fashion-forward consumers to the mainstream, a trend must be modified to make it more acceptable. The process sometimes dilutes the look so much that it loses its stylistic integrity. The novelty disappears, taking with it the original appeal.

In the case of a fad that has been identified and labeled, demand can become frenzied. If the coattail or bandwagon effect is too successful too fast, overproduction can result in rapid saturation of the market. The fad runs its course and collapses, leaving inventory but no buyers. Saturation can occur with any trend—when a trend moves into the mainstream and is seen widely, fashion-forward consumers have already moved on. Eventually most consumers have had a chance to see, accept, or reject the trend, and begin looking for something new.

Self-limiting factors, excess, loss of stylistic integrity, and saturation signal the end of a fad (or the longer-lived fashion) (Meyersohn & Katz, 1957). To anticipate the end, look at:

- The function the fad (fashion) serves. Yogawear builds on the popularity of this form of fitness but easily translates to the lifestyles of all comfort seekers.
- The fad (fashion) as symbolic of the spirit of the times. Love beads symbolized hippie times, wide-shouldered suits identified women entering the workplace, and low-rise jeans signaled a toned sexiness. When times change, so does the symbol.

Recognizing barriers to acceptance, assessing possible modifications to extend the fad, and judging the effect of those modifications on stylistic integrity are part of trend management.

Trend Management

Consumers develop relationships with style, products, and brands based on habit, familiarity, and satisfaction. For a new trend to succeed, it must often replace a current purchase pattern. Managers act on both sides of the process—one set attempting to shore up the established trend with new and improved versions, the other attempting to break the old pattern and start a new one. In both cases, managers must be sensitive to consumer and media networks, understand how they work, and recognize when they must be stimulated to gain competitive advantage (Farrell, 1998).

Managerial decisions are affected by three classes of change:

- Short-term variations, such as the path of trends as they emerge, evolve, and dissipate.
- Cyclical variations, as when style features repeat over time in response to an underlying trend.
- Long-term trends, when there are fundamental and continuous changes in the pattern of culture.

Understanding how trends develop and move through society provides the perspective that managers need to shape the decision-making process.

TREND ANALYSIS AND SYNTHESIS

Many variations of apparel styles are available in the marketplace simultaneously. Almost all are "marked" with meaning. An unmarked apparel item is the most generic of its kind. When color or styling is added, the apparel becomes a marker for some identity. Think of a white T-shirt. How many meanings can be attached to a simple white T-shirt depending on the way it is worn, its fit, what it is paired with, and the occasion when it is worn? People are symbol users and apparel offers a stage for that ability.

Each person—female or male—must make decisions about what styles to pluck from the marketplace for personal use. These decisions include those about hair, cosmetics, clothing, and accessories. Being antifashion or "no-fashion" is as much a decision as being fashionable. People make these decisions every day when they dress. Because the decisions are based partly on demographics, lifestyle, and situation and partly on personality and taste, a certain consistency emerges for each individual—a personal signature style.

People in all likelihood are a member of a **style tribe** because of where they live, how they make a living, or how they choose to spend their leisure time. Groups evolve a way of dressing that signals the group's identity and aesthetic code.

Because there exists an almost infinite universe of style variations, the possibilities for individual expression and group identification are also infinite. Yet people's styles can be classified into general categories. Combining styles under an umbrella definition makes it possible for designers to act as style tribe leaders, specialty stores to develop retail concepts that appeal to certain customers and not to others, and marketers to target a specific consumer audience. Marketers call these classification schemes **consumer segmentation**.

Analysis and synthesis are the two faces of forecasting. In **analysis**, a phenomenon is dissected to achieve a more complete understanding of its components. **Synthesis** is a creative reintegration of the parts. In fashion forecasting that means:

- An accurate reading of the trend in all its subtle aspects.
- Matching the trend with the consumer segment most likely to adopt it initially.
- Matching the trend with the product category, price point, and retail concept most likely to complement it.

Finally, the forecaster hypothesizes about what it will take to energize and accelerate the flow of the trend across consumer segments.

Consumer Segmentation

Once upon a time (not long ago), a trend moved from a few fashion-forward consumers to the mainstream (the majority of consumers). But does the mainstream even exist anymore? Most trends today move within niches, few are picked up by the majority of consumers (Haber, 2007b). So now, more than ever, forecasters and other fashion industry professionals must pay careful attention to the definitions of market niches. The terms **consumer segment** and **target audience** have thus far been used in a general way to mean that certain people are more likely than others to adopt an innovation at a particular time in the diffusion process. For marketers, these terms have a more precise meaning. An editor describing the profile of the magazine's readers, advertising executives describing the consumers most likely to relate to an ad campaign, designers talking about the kind of person most likely to buy their collections—all these executives are describing the target audience. A target audience is that slice of the population most likely to be attracted to the tangible and intangible attributes of a product, company image, or service. Defining the target audience takes discipline. It is much easier to think that every person between the ages of 25 and 45 will want a particular product or identify with a certain image. However, attempting to hit a target audience that's too inclusive results in creating indistinct, unfocused, generic merchandise without differentiation from other similar products in the market. Achieving **differentiation** means presenting a product in a way that highlights how it is different and better than other products of its type.

Traditionally a target audience would be defined as one or more consumer segments, each with certain demographic characteristics such as age, gender, ethnicity, and income. Then, the marketing executive develops a **positioning** strategy (Ries & Trout, 1986), a unique marketing approach that:

- Appeals directly to that target audience.
- Differentiates the product from all others in the category.
- Positions the product in the minds of the consumers as desirable for purchase (Figure 2.12).

Segmentation strategies based on **demographics**—consumer characteristics such as age, gender, marital status, and occupation—are

Figure 2.12.
Eileen Fisher (*above*), whose designs have a distinctive look positioned to appeal to women of a certain age with flattering, modern styling without fussy, distracting details (*right*). (*WWD*, Courtesy of Fairchild Publications)

no longer effective because consumer attitudes and behavior are not driven primarily by demographics. Sometimes a product crosses boundaries by appealing to consumers in wide demographic categories but to only a small number of people overall—for example, technical fabrics for active sports crossing over into casual wear. Consumers can behave in unexpected ways—for example, when very affluent consumers combine luxury branded goods from specialty stores and basics from discount retailers. Some of today's consumers still ride the trend waves of fashion but others are decidedly antifashion. Shifts in consumer behavior mean that the traditional way of doing business whereby manufacturers propose new products, identify targets for those products through a segmentation study, and develop a positioning strategy is too simplistic for today's marketplace.

Psychographics—consumer psychology plus demographics—help identify a consumer segment by shared values, attitudes, preferences, and behaviors (Piirto, 1991). Psychographics evolved from groundwork laid in the late 1950s when characteristics such as personality traits, attitudes, and motives were used to identify consumer clusters. By the mid-1960s, nondemographic segmentation was becoming a keystone in marketing strategy. Today, marketers view the value system embedded in each individual—the consumer's culture—as having more impact than demographics.

The consumer's culture can overrule demographic classifications. High-income households consider brand quality to be more important than do consumers at lower income levels. Yet consumers of all income levels who tend to be trendsetters or opinion leaders show a far greater preference for quality than even

● ● ● activity 2.7. **Charting Fashion Labels**
Using highlighter pens, identify labels attached to trends, apparel items, and fashion looks in a recent fashion magazine. Develop a dictionary of names, labels, or slogans associated with current fashion in a notebook. Jot down additional ones as you read fashion magazines from now on. Over time, this dictionary of fashion labels will chart the emergence, diffusion, dominance, and eclipse of fashion trends.

high-income families (Kelly, 1994). Health-, fitness-, and nutrition-conscious consumers comprise a relatively small but influential segment of consumers in all demographic categories. Although they may be of different ages and come from various income ranges, they are more alike than different when it comes to choosing products that enhance and support their image of themselves as healthy and fit. Positioning becomes more actionable when it is built on both the "whos"—demographics—and the "whys"—psychographics—of consumer behavior (Rueff, 1991).

Geodemographics links geography and demographics to show the clustering of similar people in a neighborhood (Edelson, 2003). Census data on age, income, ethnicity, and other categories are "smoothed out" to create an identity, label, and affluence rating for a neighborhood. The resulting clusters are useful for pinpointing locations for new stores or malls, to target mailings of catalogs, and to reveal insights about consumer preferences. The fragmentation of markets in the 1980s meant that products and services must be targeted not to a mass market but to submarkets identified by combinations of demographics and geography.

In the early 1970s, a college professor and entrepreneur used cluster analysis and census data to create zip code clusters (Weiss, 1988). The concept behind the analysis is that neighborhoods geographically separated may be more similar to each other than those nearby. For example, the demographic makeup of college towns and the preferences of the residents are similar no matter where in the country they are located. These college towns are more like each other than they are like other towns in their vicinity. Using this logic, the company Claritas merged U.S. Census data with credit card, mail-order sales, television viewing, subscription, and other purchasing information to create PRIZM (Potential Rating Index by Zip Market)—a system sorting all the zip codes in the United States into neighborhood types. Each type can be profiled by demographics, lifestyle, media usage, and preference for make of car, food, and other products. The data are updated each year (Levanas, 1998). Married couples with children, who are seen as affluent, living in the suburbs, or in new subdivisions—categorized as "Kids & Cul-de-Sacs"—make up a diverse segment of the population, and include high percentages of Hispanic and Asian Americans. They can be expected to make expenditures for child-centered products and services, shop at the Disney Store, eat at Chuck E. Cheese, watch Nickelodeon TV, and read parenting magazines. Singles in their twenties—"Up & Comers"—live in second-tier cities and are mostly recent college grads. Their interests center on athletics, technology, and nightlife. PRIZM currently has 66 defined consumer segments (Edwards, 2007).

Claritas was one of the first companies to make geodemographic information useful to marketing executives, but it has been joined by others so that today's executive can choose among competing firms. One of the key questions in using geodemographics is how to define a neighborhood—by zip code or by census track? Each company offers its own version of clustering and its own interpretation of the resulting clusters.

Today's executive is not restricted to buying geodemographic analysis from one of the research firms. The technology is now available on the executive's desktop. While the basic technology linking census data and mapping has been around since the 1960s, the software did not become available on the personal computer until the mid-1990s (Freed, 1994). At that time, companies began to sell the basic mapping software at a relatively low price, planning to make money by selling updated packages of geographic, economic, and demographic data. With the software in place, an analyst can map competitor locations, areas of dense population, neighborhoods with high income and high-traffic roads, and other information to support strategic marketing decisions.

Geodemographics is useful to forecasters in pinpointing the markets where hot trends begin and in mapping their potential diffusion. Geodemographics can identify the towns and neighborhoods that are teen-poor (under 4 percent of the population is aged 14 to 17) and those with higher concentrations for teens, areas that are attracting young adults, and those where boomers are migrating (Sutton, 1993). These patterns signal retail growth potential for some stores and product categories and a mismatch for others. Because the United States is heading for a more diverse population by the end of the twenty-first century, one way to forecast the future is to identify and monitor locations where diversity already exists (Allen & Turner, 1990). Geodemographics allows forecasters to locate diverse neighborhoods where consumption patterns today may anticipate those that will develop in other locales as the future unfolds.

GENERATIONAL COHORTS

Similarity in patterns of consumer behavior have been traced to **generational cohorts** who share the same "age location" in history and a collective mind-set (Strauss & Howe, 1991). In this view, group membership is involuntary, permanent, and finite—from birth on, all members encounter the same events, moods, and trends at similar ages, giving each cohort a distinct biography and a peer personality. Individuals in the cohort may agree with the values and viewpoints of their generation or spend a lifetime battling against it; either way, membership in the cohort shapes their relationship to people and products. Using this typology, five generational cohorts are currently active consumers (Gronbach, 2008).

The G.I. Generation

Born between 1901 and 1924, the G.I. generation lived through the Great Depression in their youth and fought in World War II (1941–1945) as young adults. Originally 70 million strong, this generation has declined to 5 million. Consumption is mostly limited to daily maintenance and health care. Their purchasing tends to be through their boomer caregivers.

The Silent Generation

Born between 1925 and 1945, the silent generation came of age during the 1950s and fought in the Korean War (1950–1953). Of the 53 million born into this generation, about 45 million remain. This group's purchasing centers on delaying aging and remaining independent, eating out, and shopping for a bargain.

The Baby Boom Generation

Born between 1946 and 1964, the children in this generation were the result of a post-World War II baby boom. Boomers were the first TV generation and fought the first televised war, in Vietnam. Instead of bonding to fight the war as the G.I. generation had, some boomers bonded to protest the war and evade service. This is the generation of Youthquake, the Summer of Love, Woodstock, and Earth Day. They can be subdivided into an older cohort who were the flower children and hippies of the late 1960s and early 1970s and a younger cohort who became the yuppies (young urban professionals) of the early 1980s. The 75 million boomers control much of the nation's wealth and retire at the rate of one every eight seconds. Whereas their purchase of cars and apparel is slowing, boomers value products that make life easier or save time.

Generation X

Born between 1965 and 1980, this generation experienced a higher risk of being children of divorce (almost twice as often as boomers) and grew up as latchkey kids and as members of blended families due to remarriage. Boomers experienced the euphoria of Youthquake, whereas Generation X-ers were labeled "slackers" for their pragmatic approach, sense of social distance, and falling expectations. The first computer generation, Gen X consumers are experienced shoppers, fond of popular culture, and cynical about media manipulation. A small generation (9 million fewer than

●●● activity 2.8. Researching the Generations

Use the generational names as keywords in a database search. What kinds of information are available on generational cohorts? Select one generation, and collect several recent articles. Analyze how the observations in the articles relate to the design and sales of apparel products.

● ● ● activity 2.9. Generations and Life Stages

Use the articles from Activity 2.8 to analyze the spending patterns for possessions as a sign of accomplishment and identity, the purchase of services, and the search for meaningful experiences for a generational cohort. Try to project the spending patterns for this generational cohort at the next life stage.

boomers), these consumers don't respond to conventional media and are difficult to target in the fragmentation of the Internet.

Millennial Generation, Generation Y

Born between 1981 and 1995, this generation's parents are mostly boomers. The size of this generation almost equals boomers and surpasses them in purchasing—Gen Y purchasing is at 500 percent compared to their parents when adjusted in dollars. Attentive to cyberspace, fickle in their tastes, and expecting the best, this group favors brands and retailers with strong ecological or humanitarian records. This is the generation that is rethinking everything and taking the fashion industry with them. Demographers aren't precise in placing dividing lines between generations but Gen Y probably ended in 2000 and a new generation, yet to be named, is being born (Tran, 2008d).

The apparel marketer must be savvy about targeting consumers by generational cohort. If it is true that the mainstream (a majority of all consumers) no longer exists, each American generation spanning roughly 20 years, encompassing millions of consumers, and shaped by unique cultural conditions provides its own mainstream with specific needs, wants, and aspirations.

Identifying generations in other cultures helps forecasters and other fashion professionals understand and define global marketing opportunities. China is likely to become the largest retail economy and the spending power will be in the hands of the "only child" generation—profiled as urban, educated, ranging from late teens to early thirties, with rising disposable incomes. The Chinese who are part of this generation grew up during boom times, embrace fashion, and enjoy spending money on themselves. Wherever a company does business, a generational view can provide insights into the marketplace (Lowther, 2008).

LIFESTYLE SEGMENTS

Psychographics was extended in the early 1970s by the introduction of research into lifestyles (Piirto, 1991). In that time, society was being remade by young people who dropped out rather than get married and start families and careers, and by women who began choosing careers over traditional homemaker roles. Lifestyle research was an attempt to understand the changing social order. The framework for such studies is Attitudes, Interests, and Opinions (AIO)—How do consumers spend their time? What interests are important to them? How do they view themselves? What opinions do they hold about the world around them?

A typical lifestyle study will survey consumers and then sort them into categories like soccer mom for stay-at-home matriarchs. But the marketing firm Consumer Eyes identified untraditional influencers—consumer groups with fluid career paths, an interest in new media, market smarts, and skill in spreading their preferences to others (Kinsey, 2007). Some of these nine lifestyle segments are:

- Karma Queens—baby boomer women who haven't lost their hippie sensibilities, respond to woman-to-woman brand appeals, show interest in products that relate to mind-body-spirit enhancement, and drive quirky automobiles.
- Denim Dads—stay-at-home dads who seek balance in work and life, spend lots of time online, and share in their kids' musical tastes.
- Ms. Independents—single women with high disposable incomes to spend on themselves who watch style and home decor shows on television, and are interested equally in high-end fashion and interior design.
- Middlemen—21- to 35-year-old men seeking a laid-back lifestyle, not seeking job advancement, are passionate gamers (video games, sports, etc.), and prefer fast-food restaurants.
- E-litists—couples who look for status and bragging rights within the "green" (environmental) movement without concern for prices, shop for organic foods and earth-friendly products, listen to National Public Radio, and drive hybrid cars.

Today, lifestyle segments form a foundation concept for product development, marketing, and merchandising. A lifestyle message has become a key strategy for apparel brands. Vendor shops in department stores present the company's products as a recognizable, coordinated concept carried out in products, accessories, display fixtures, mannequins, construction materials, and ambiance ("One-stop shops," 1998). Consumers recognize products and presentation as belonging to their group and gravitate toward those brands.

LIFE STAGES

Similarity in patterns of consumer behavior can be traced to the life stage of the consumer. Consumption priorities alter depending on the stage of life and the accompanying tasks and challenges. Using life stages as a framework, the forecaster can predict shifts in what consumers do with their discretionary dollars.

Adults at every life stage blend all three kinds of consumption, but each life stage puts a different priority on the elements in the combination. A young couple starting life together and beginning careers will put emphasis on acquiring possessions and defining their image as individuals and as a family. Spending focuses on a car, a media center, and a home or an apartment with furnishings. Financial security dampens the need for acquiring possessions but fuels the satisfaction of personal, entertainment, and convenience needs through the purchase of services. Spending focuses on season tickets to the theater or sporting events, travel, restaurant meals, and professional services such as custom clothing, personal shoppers, lawn maintenance, and interior design services. With gratification of the need for possessions and services, the consumer shifts emphasis to altruistic activities such as charity work or mentoring others, personally meaningful experiences, and life-enhancing pastimes.

The life stages represent consumption of different products and the pursuit of different kinds of experience. Although the stages are related to maturing, consumers at all ages participate in each kind of spending. Only the emphasis shifts and with it, the consumer's discretionary spending.

Figure 2.13.
A fractal such as the Sierpinski gasket shows the growth pattern generated by self-similarity from a single shape to a three-dimensional version. In the same way, a single individual's demographic and psychographic profile can be aggregated with similar individuals to form consumer segments with certain degrees of self-similarity.

FORECASTER'S TOOLBOX: VISUALIZING TARGET MARKETS

Describing a "market of one"—one individual consumer—and a consumer segment is like describing a fractal. Fractal geometry is based on the unifying concept that self-similarity occurs regardless of changes in scale (Figure 2.13). The broken edges of a rock and the shape of the mountain it came from are similar in composition and fracture pattern even though the difference in scale is enormous. This insight has enabled scientists to understand and describe many phenomena in the natural world, from the way a fern adds leaves to the shape of coastlines seen from space (Schroeder, 1991).

Consumer segmentation has the same underlying self-similarity because the pattern builds up from individuals with certain demographic and psychographic characteristics, representatives of a certain lifestyle segment, and confronting a specific life stage. The individuals blend into groups and into larger consumer segments based on shared characteristics (Piirto, 1991). The consumer segmentation strategies for the twenty-first century reflect the new realities of consumer behavior—there is still an underlying similarity among consumers who gravitate to a particular style or image, but that similarity is complex and multifaceted. Forecasters use cohort membership, lifestyle, and life stage to project potential acceptance or rejection of trends and styles.

Key Terms and Concepts

Analysis	Geodemographics
Backcast	Hype
Buzz	Influentials
Change agents	Information
Coattail effect	cascade
Compatibility	Innovation
Complexity	Innovators
Consumer	Labeling
adoption	Legitimation
process	Mainstream
Consumer	Memes
segment	Observability
Consumer	Opinion leaders
segmentation	Perceived risk
Demographics	Popular culture
Differentiation	Positioning
Diffusion curve	Primary sources
Diffusion process	Psychographics
Dissonance	Relative advantage
Distant opinion	S-curve
leader	Social risk
Economic risk	Style tribes
Enjoyment risk	Synthesis
Evolution of a	Target audience
trend	Tastemakers
Fashion leaders	Trialability
Flow	Two-step flow
Gatekeepers	Viral marketing
Generational	Word-of-mouth
cohorts	

Discussion Questions

Introducing a new product, ways to combine apparel pieces, or sensibility about clothing is an incredibly risky and complicated business. Consumers play many different roles and have many decision points in the process. Understanding how an innovation spreads provides a framework for forecasting because it suggests what to watch and where to do the observing. Use the following questions to summarize and review this chapter.

Diffusion of innovation: What filters do forecasters use in evaluating the potential of an innovation based on its characteristics? How does the consumer adoption process interact with the characteristics of an innovation to produce an approach or avoidance behavior? What risks does a consumer face when deciding to adopt an innovation? What is the life cycle of a fad? How does that differ from the life cycle of a fashion or a classic? Who acts as fashion change agents? What is the role of a fashion change agent?

Defining trends: How do trends evolve and move in society? How have trends evolved to shape fashion at the beginning of the twenty-first century?

Consumer segmentation: What is the difference between target audience and consumer segment? How does a purchaser's generational membership define preferences? How does life stage influence the purchasing behavior of consumers?

Additional Forecasting Activities

Missing Links. Even with the abundance of apparel products in the market, consumers do not always find what they are looking for. Interview consumers from each generational segment—G.I., silents, boomers, Gen Xers, and Gen Yers. What styles, features, or characteristics are missing from the apparel marketplace? These voids in the market represent opportunities for extending diffusion of innovation to new consumer groups or creating new products.

Different lifestyles side by side. Compare the lifestyle characteristics of the college community with towns nearby. Investigate lifestyle characteristics such as median age, income levels, educational attainment, size of families, and employment. Do a "walkaround survey" of the shops and the style and price range of merchandise in each town. Prepare guidelines for merchandise assortment based on lifestyle characteristics for each town.

Listening to consumers. Convene a series of panel discussions with people at different life stages. Prepare a set of questions to find out about the priorities these consumer have for possessions, the purchase of services, and experiences. What are the implications for apparel companies based on your analysis of these discussions?

Resource Pointers

Consumer Research:

Claritas Inc. (consumer segmentation): www.claritas.com

Yankelovich (consumer segmentation): www.yankelovich.com

Age Wave, Inc. (consumers over 50): www.agewave.com

TRU (Teenage Research Unlimited): www.teenresearch.com

The Intelligence Group / Youth Intelligence: www.youthintelligence.com

The paradox of fashion is that everyone is trying at the same time to be like, and to be unlike, his fellow-men.

—J. C. Flugel

3
THE DIRECTION OF FASHION CHANGE

OBJECTIVES

- Identify the directional theories of fashion change—their source, basic tenets, and predictive power.
- Cultivate skills in analyzing current fashion within a theoretical framework.
- Increase awareness of visualization as a tool of analysis and communication.

Fashion Movement

Trend watching is a diversion enjoyed by many. Even a casual trend watcher will see discernable patterns. At some point in time, people begin to feel that wearing colorful clothes is unsophisticated and that black is "cool." Closets fill up with neutrals until, seemingly overnight, black looks drab and monotonous. A creative street fashion or a fashion runway fills up with pink and suddenly color seems fresh and inviting. Every aspect of fashion, from color to the length of skirts, the shape of the silhouette, or the placement of pockets, is in constant motion.

Anyone can pick up on a trend when it lands in the mailbox trumpeted in magazine headlines complete with an eight-page photographic spread. For the fashion professional, recognizing a trend at that stage means that it is almost too late to use the information for competitive advantage. Instead, fashion executives look for competitive advantage by identifying trends early. To do that, they must position themselves in the most likely spots to watch for emerging trends. With experience, a trend watcher becomes skilled at spotting the elusive and subtle shifts that signal fashion change.

Observation is not enough. If the trend watcher is to take advantage, they need a framework for explaining how the trend began and its likely path within a social system. The directional theories of fashion change make prediction easier by pointing to the likely starting points for a fashion trend, the expected direction that trend will take, and how long the trend will last.

As with fashion itself, the theories that explain fashion movement are constantly revised and refined. The fashion forecaster's toolbox contains all the explanations and recognized patterns that have explained past fashion and can be used to arrange and order current observations. Social scientists continue to seek better explanations and to suggest new theories of fashion change. The forecaster uses the theories by matching observations with the explanation that best fits and then projecting the next stage.

Visualizing the most likely pattern of change is the first step toward prediction. Abstracting a theory into a visual representation clarifies the situation and aids in analyzing what comes next. Visualizations—a layer cake with each layer representing a stratum of the marketplace or the formation of a fashion wave—help explain the concepts and communicate the logic of predictions to others.

Trend watching executives move in the social world observing, categorizing what they see, and matching that to the preferences and behavior of consumers. These fashion professionals seem to make their decisions "from their gut" in a mysteriously intuitive process. Actually, that intuitive response is the result of a highly developed sensitivity to the social environment plus the almost instant application of one of the forecasting frameworks. Experience and application of the best explanations cannot guarantee success—the situation is too complex for absolute accuracy in prediction. However, preparation and practice can improve the odds for professional trend watchers.

The Direction of Fashion Change

The three directional theories of fashion change predict that fashion will either trickle down, trickle up, or trickle across consumer segments. Introduced at different times during the twentieth century, these theories reflect not only a general understanding of fashion dynamics but also the specific marketplace conditions at the time they were proposed. Each theory has been criticized and revised since its introduction but remains a valuable guide in explaining fashion leadership and predicting fashion movement. The directional theories of fashion change help fashion professionals answer the questions: Where do fashion innovations begin? Who leads and who follows? How quickly will a fashion move through society? When will a style reach the end of its popularity?

TRICKLE-DOWN THEORY

Imagine a fashion observer living at the turn of the twentieth century. How would they explain fashion? Looking backward, the observer sees that past fashion was dictated by the nobility who were leaders in all areas of fashionable behavior by birthright, rank, and wealth. Fashion spread slowly downward through the class structure but never reached all levels. The lower classes did not have the income, access, or freedom to follow fashion's dictates. Looking around at their own time, the observer notices that fashion is still restricted to those at the top of the class structure—the rich and socially prominent. The Industrial Revolution has made possible the building of great fortunes and the display of wealth through fashionable possessions including homes, furnishings, art, and handcrafted fashion. This period, roughly 1900 to 1914, is known as *la Belle Époque* in France, the Edwardian period in England, and the Gilded Age in America. It was characterized by women wearing extravagant, elaborate fashions that required devotion, attention, and seriousness at both the acquisition stage and in wearing the clothes in everyday life.

Veblen (1899) was one such observer at the turn of the 20th century. He described the upper strata of the social system as the leisure class. Members of the leisure class displayed wealth in two distinctive ways, through **conspicuous leisure** and **conspicuous consumption**. A person who does not have to work for a living and participates in an extravagant lifestyle of travel, entertainment, and the pursuit of pleasure demonstrates conspicuous leisure. Philanthropy, art collecting, acquisition of homes and furnishings, and apparel with expensive modes of production and materials demonstrate conspicuous consumption. In both these models, wealth serves as the background for the activities that were the hallmark of the times.

The Origins of the Theory

Explaining fashion movement in such an era is relatively easy: fashion moves downward from the elite class to the lower classes in stately and slow progression. But the explanation is not complete until it explains not only what happens but why. Simmel (1904), a sociologist, identified the engine of fashion change in the opposing human tendencies toward conformity and individuality. No aspect of life can satisfy the demands of these two opposing principles, but social life and fashion offer a perfect battleground where striving for social adaptation and the need of differentiation can be played out.

The dual tendencies can be displayed when one person's style is toward imitation and another's is toward differentiation. The imitator believes in social similarity, in acting like others. The individual seeking differentiation constantly experiments with the new, relying in large part on personal convictions. These dual drives can also function in social groups where fashion simultaneously functions as a means of class distinction and as a badge of group uniformity.

Simmel observed three stages, as follows: (1) the elite class differentiated itself through fashion; (2) the adjacent lower classes imitated the look; and (3) the elite class moved to adopt a new fashion in an attempt to maintain the differentiation. These stages occur in social forms, apparel, aesthetic judgment, and the whole style of human expression—a view that expands consideration of fashion change from simply apparel to a broader range of activities and behaviors. Simmel described the constant movement between the three stages as a game that "goes merrily on."

Because the motivation to fit in and stand out can never fully or finally be gratified, fashion change is inevitable for the individual and for the social group. Simmel explained that the distinctiveness afforded by newness in the early stages of a fashion is destroyed by its spread to imitators until the fashion wanes and dies. Simmel concluded that the charm of fashion lay in its novelty coupled with its transitory nature.

The views of Veblen and Simmel form the framework for the **trickle-down theory** of fashion change. The theory identified:

- The source of fashion ideas—designers who catered to wealthy clients with a taste for conspicuous consumption and the leisure to pursue fashion.
- The fashion leaders—those fashionable and highly visible individuals who served as models for the new looks.
- The direction of fashion change—downward from the elite class to the next adjacent class.
- The speed of change—regulated by the ability of the lower classes to see, obtain, and copy the fashion.
- The dynamics of change—the pursuit of the dual drives for differentiation and imitation.

Criticism and Revision of the Theory

Fashion observers in the latter half of the twentieth century have criticized the trickle-down theory as being flawed. The chief criticism is that the elite did not consistently set prevailing styles any time after the introduction of mass production and mass communication (Banner, 1983; Blumer, 1969; Lowe & Lowe, 1984). McCracken (1988a) points out that the theory oversimplifies the social system. Instead of just two or three layers with the elite at the top, the social system actually has many layers simultaneously engaged in differentiation and imitation.

McCracken also questioned visualization of the process as trickle down because the impetus for change comes from the subordinate classes as they hunt for the **status markers** of the upper class. He proposed replacing trickle down with **chase and flight**—chase because fashion change was driven by the imitators who chased the status markers of the elite in a drive toward upward social mobility; flight because the elite responded to imitation by flying away toward new forms of differentiation. Although this new visualization neatly captures the dynamics of the process, the phrase did not catch on with fashion writers, who still use the earlier trickle-down image.

Along with the criticism came some proposed revisions to the theory. Behling (1985 / 1986) identified a new, highly visible upper class made up of those occupying power positions in business, politics, and media. As she points out, "they are Veblen's new conspicuous consumer . . . from whom, under particular circumstances, fashion trickles down."

Simon-Miller (1985) pointed out that the fashionable elite in the latter half of the twentieth century practiced a kind of status denial—people with the wealth and status to wear anything they wished chose to dress down. Instead of conspicuous consumption, this variation was called **reverse ostentation** or **conspicuous counterconsumption**, but it served the same purpose—differentiation. Dressing down by the fashionable elite became news in 1993 when magazines lambasted celebrities about "style-free" dressing in shapeless T-shirts and denim, thrift shop finds, and "farm-wife dresses." As one actress put it, when you see people with real power dressing down, it must be the thing to do.

Interestingly, Simmel (1904) described the same phenomenon in his time. He characterized two distinctive fashion types:

- The fashion victims (whom he termed "dudes") in whom "the social demands of fashion appear exaggerated to such a degree that they completely assume an individualistic and peculiar character."
- The antifashion individual, whose "conscious neglect of fashion represents similar imitation, but under an inverse sign."

In both these types Simmel saw a commonality—both types are paying homage to the power of fashion, one in the form of exaggeration, the other, by consciously attempting to ignore it. Simmel said that both these types exhibit a "tendency toward individual conspicuousness."

More recently economists have used seeking status as the basis for explaining fashion change. Pesendorfer (1995, 2004, 2005) sees fashion as having no intrinsic value other than its power to signal status. High-status items remain "in" only so long as their signal strength is strong. Pesendorfer's novel contribution is to point out the active role of manufacturers and retailers who manipulate the price (either to maintain the high status with high prices or to take advantage of weakening strength by lowering prices to increase sales to wider audiences) and who time the introduction of new high-status items. Coelho and McClure (1993) emphasized that fashion professionals recognize status-seeking behavior and use "prestige pricing" to create "snob" appeal for a product. Fritjers (1998) did not place the power to create high-status goods in the hands of the producer but instead in the status seeker. Not every high-priced, limited-production item becomes a status symbol—only those selected by the wealthy, fashion-forward consumer. That buyer selects those items likely to maintain a high price and power as a status symbol for some time in the future. Like others seeking to explain the trickle-down movement of fashion, these theorists see desire for conspicuousness as expressed in status symbols as the beginning and widespread availability as the end of an item's life cycle.

Forecaster's Toolbox: Theory in Action

Can the trickle-down theory of fashion movement be useful to a fashion forecaster today? People's motivations to participate in fashion remain essentially the same no matter the century. The trickle-down theory underscores the self-perpetuating cycle based on people's basic human tendencies toward imitation and differentiation. People still feel pressure to adapt to their place in society's structure and to the rules of their narrower circle, while simultaneously seeking to affirm their individuality. And the field of fashion is still an excellent battleground for these two opposing tendencies to be played out.

Status Symbols: "In" or "Out"?

Veblen's observations about the need that some people have for conspicuous consumption continues to be part of the fashion picture even if this is more prominent in some decades than in others. Conspicuous consumption was "in" when yuppies were ascendant in the 1980s, but a stock crash late in the decade ushered in a period that shunned ostentation in the early 1990s. By mid-decade consumers were once again in the mood to treat themselves to status symbols. That feeling ended with a downturn in the economy that coincided with the national trauma of 9/11 (Bird, 1995; Seckler, 2002a). The economy rebounded for a time, but by the mid-2000s high energy costs and slipping home prices once again sent the economy reeling. Fashion responded with "the

reassurance trend," defined as classic styles and appropriateness, and consumers became careful spenders (Beckett, 2007).

The accessory category is most immune to the ups and downs of the economy. Shoppers can be segmented into true luxury shoppers who shop exclusively for name brands in upscale stores, aspirational shoppers who seek status by buying a piece of a designer label, and the brand-centric who, like trophy hunters, buy a particular brand wherever they find it (Daswani, 2008). But dropping consumer confidence can reduce the appeal of even status handbags— those with designer labels, recognizable styling, and prices around $1,000. In a down economy even luxury shoppers feel "It bag" fatigue (Wilson, 2007e). The desire for status symbols follows the cyclical nature of the economy and brands that are strong in one upturn may not be preferred in the next.

The Shifting Power of Status Markers

The theory predicts that status markers can lose power when they become too available to all consumers. Take, for example, the Van Cleef & Arpels Alhambra line—quatrefoil, clover-shaped charms introduced in the 1960s but not discovered and popularized by celebrities until the early 2000s. Original earrings retail for $1,200, but necklaces with diamond-covered clovers can sell for over $60,000. Attempting to stave off saturation of the market, Van Cleef extended the line by combining large and small clovers and by adding heart, leaf, and butterfly shapes. But by the mid-2000s, knockoffs of the designs appeared in stores and online for as little as $50. To each woman, the clovers are a badge of status and inclusion, but when that badge is seen on celebrities and in the street, real and fake, ubiquity becomes the kiss of death (Kuczynski, 2007).

Quality Issues in Conspicuous Consumption

Nystrom (1928) constructed a business rule based on Veblen's ideas: "to succeed as a fashion, [a style] must have qualities that advertise either conspicuous leisure or conspicuous consumption for the user." He also elaborated on the description of those exercising fashion leadership to include not only people with wealth and the power to use it but also those who know how to use it artistically and recognize this artistic ability in others. These extensions of Veblen's ideas provide the fashion forecaster with more specification in applying the ideas of the trickle-down theory to observations of today's marketplace.

Fashion leadership is tied to more than price; it is about taste and quality. To most consumers, the $99 "It bag" knockoff is indistinguishable from the $1,000 original. To buyers with more discriminating tastes, the workmanship, quality of the leather, findings, and finishes on the expensive bag make it authentic and worth the price. Just as some buyers appreciate the beauty and heft of a gold Alhambra necklace at $12,900, others are pleased to have the look in yellow gold-plated metal for $50. After the symbol is usurped by those without the ability to recognize the artistry, the symbol becomes less appealing to the connoisseurs who were early adopters of the look (Agins, 1994a).

Groups Worth Watching

There are two problems for the fashion forecaster in applying the trickle-down theory to today's society: (1) the multiplication of layers in the social system since the theory was first proposed; and (2) the difficulty in identifying the elite. Simmel's formulation specified only two layers—an elite striving for differentiation, and a lower class imitating that elite. The twentieth

century has produced a rising standard of living for many more people and stratified society into many more status layers than in Simmel's day. Each of these layers undertakes fashion change for the purposes of imitation and differentiation (McCracken, 1988a). The result is a much more complex dynamic. The top layer is concerned only with differentiation, the bottom layer only with imitation, but the intermediate layers simultaneously imitate the layer above and seek differentiation from the layer below. McCracken sees this complexity as raising additional questions: Are some groups more imitative than others are? Are there aggressively imitative groups that move so fast that differentiation is not a concern? Are some groups more concerned with differentiation? Are some groups so concerned about differentiation that they create fashion rather than imitate a higher-level group?

At first McCracken's questions seem to complicate the forecaster's job because it seems logical that a multilayered system requires more monitoring than a simpler one. However, identifying groups most likely to generate fashion change actually directs the forecaster's attention and narrows the job of monitoring the system. Because the forecaster cannot watch every layer, why not watch instead for instabilities where fashion activity is intense and fast-paced?

Fast-Paced Differentiation

These groups are more likely to feed the system with fashion change because they are most concerned with using fashion for differentiation. They may be the elite, high-status group in a particular stratum of the society or part of the new visible elite highlighted by media attention. As a group, these fashion innovators are likely to create ripples through surrounding groups, setting off a chain of fashion changes.

Take, for example, the niche "upscale streetwear" that appeals to "style-conscious young men with an aversion to mall culture." Looking for self-expression and self-invention through distinctive styling, hard-to-replicate details, quality construction, and trends with a short life span, they hunt for little-known labels in trendy stores, alternative magazines, fashion blogs, and specially targeted Web sites. In this world, "talk of coveted new merchandise races like a current" through the network. Much of the payoff comes from "owning something you had to hunt down." For this group of fashion devotees, exclusivity and scarcity is the key: "We all know what Ralph Lauren does, what Tommy Hilfiger does. What we want is an artist's piece" (La Ferla, 2006).

Aggressive Imitation

Although some groups specialize in rapid style differentiation, feeding ideas into the fashion system, of equal interest to the fashion forecaster are the fast-moving imitative groups. Some teens and young adult groups imitate sports figures or other fashion icons, rapidly picking up on fashion looks or product identification and just as rapidly moving on to the next big thing. In such groups, fashion interest is high. Individuals are highly sensitive to the symbolic nuances of products, use them artistically, and recognize their artistic use by others. Groups that adopt these same looks after they have been discarded by the fast-moving imitative groups are much less likely to be as sensitive to the details.

Fashion and Social Instability

Fashion exists where there is "fluidity" in the social system (Flugel, 1930). Kaiser (1990) suggested updating the theory by examining the underlying instabilities that exist in society. She identified the source of these instabilities in tensions among

cultural categories, specifically in areas of gender, ethnicity, age, and attractiveness.

gender. Androgyny, gender bending, and **gender blending** have been potent sources for fashion. From the pants-wearing athleticism of Amelia Earhart in the 1930s to the gender ambiguity of a movie like *Kinky Boots* (2005), the line between masculine and feminine in fashion has grown blurry.

ethnicity. Although the debate about the salability of fashion magazines that feature African-American models seems dated, the controversy arose again in 2008 when the July issue of Italian *Vogue* reversed the general pattern and used only black models. Steven Meisel, the photographer, cast the approximately 100 pages of photographs using well-known faces from earlier fashion eras (Pat Cleveland, Naomi Campbell, Tyra Banks) and current models. The editor, Franca Sozzani, who has steered the magazine toward coverage of art and ideas, said she was aware that the lack of diversity on runways and in magazines had created a debate within the industry (Horyn, 2008). At the same time, runways, advertising campaigns, and editorial pages of fashion magazines featured a wide range of models from other ethnic groups.

age. With the aging of a large generational cohort, the baby boomers, definitions of attractiveness as they relate to age will be more open to redefinition than in previous decades. Brands use celebrities in their forties, fifties, and sixties as spokeswomen in ads, sometimes replacing faces in their twenties. Michael Kors explained that the fashion ideal didn't jibe with the real women who buy clothes—"the simple truth is, financially, you will have more customers who are over forty" and the market can't ignore a large demographic group with high discretionary income (Karimzadeh, 2006).

attractiveness. Women with exaggerated features and idiosyncratic styles who would not previously have been considered attractive enough for modeling assignments achieved prominence. Billed as edgy and modern, these models became symbols in a time of multiculturalism. Models and actresses were also breaking other stereotypes of attractiveness such as thinness. Thinness itself became a global controversy in the mid-2000s. Reacting to criticism about the use of ultra-thin models, the fashion industry began setting guidelines based on body mass index that excluded some models from the runway (Jones, 2007b). On the other end of the scale, Steven Meisel cast a full-figure model in the all-black Italian *Vogue* issue, saying, "What's the deal with her? She's great and she's sexy" (Horyn, 2008).

Just as the instability of a more rigid class structure and the quest of lower classes for upward mobility led to the dynamics observed by Veblen and Simmel at the turn of the twentieth century, cultural instabilities surrounding gender, ethnicity, age, and attractiveness fuel fashion change today. Simmel's engine of fashion change—imitation and differentiation—is still at work in the twenty-first century as it was at the beginning of the twentieth century.

Linking the Visible Elite to a Target Audience

Identifying the elite in today's society presents a problem. There is no longer a single source of fashion leadership even among the fashionable elite. Instead, there are many highly visible public figures, some using the strategy of conspicuous consumption, some using conspicuous counterconsumption. The fashion forecaster can use this phenomenon to their advantage by linking particular celebrity cohorts with the audience most likely to admire their style and imitate at least some of their characteristics.

A few celebrities are perennial favorites appealing to a broad audience. Many are influential only for a short time, depending on their current roles. Some celebrities are influential to only a niche market that, although smaller, may be termed a desirable demographic. Buyers in their teens and twenties are considered desirable demographics because they are in an acquisitive stage in life with discretionary dollars to spend. Today's fashion forecaster has to be astute about segmenting celebrity influence, monitoring it for fashion direction, and mapping its impact on consumers.

Applying the Theory in Today's Marketplace

The real predictive power in a theory derives from its ability to clearly establish the source, the mechanism, the tempo, and the direction of fashion change (Figure 3.1). The trickle-down theory provides the fashion forecaster with the tools of the trade—an early warning system for identifying the next new thing and a paradigm for mapping out the direction and speed of fashion change. The early warning system involves identifying and monitoring:

- The visible elite.
- The status markers most likely to be imitated.
- The consumer segments most likely to imitate.
- The feeder groups for fashion ideas—that is, groups so concerned about differentiation that they create fashion rather than imitate a higher-level group.

Figure 3.1.
Trickle-down theory
of fashion change.

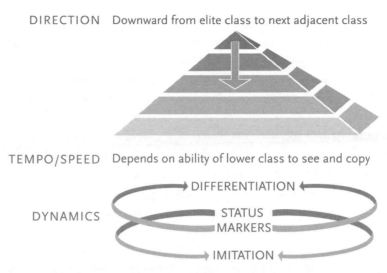

DIRECTION Downward from elite class to next adjacent class

TEMPO/SPEED Depends on ability of lower class to see and copy

DYNAMICS

DIFFERENTIATION
STATUS
MARKERS
IMITATION

SOURCE OF FASHION IDEAS Designers who propose innovation, elite as gatekeepers

SOURCE OF CHANGE Imitators

- The aggressively imitative groups moving so fast through looks that differentiation is not a concern because others often imitate these groups.
- The instabilities in the social system in terms of economic conditions, gender, ethnicity, age, and attractiveness.

Step one is observation: identifying potential fashion change. Step two is analysis: mapping the potential change to consumer segments most likely to adapt the change to their own fashion purpose. The paradigm calls for imitation to begin in adjacent groups and spread from group to group. The speed of change can be inferred from the power of the elite and the desirability and visibility of the status marker to the imitating group.

One point of observation is bloggers. A few **fashion blogs** emerged as important enough for their creators to receive invitations to designer shows ("Memo pad," 2007). They are much faster at disseminating news when compared to traditional media like magazines—bloggers can see a runway show, comment on it, and provide video feeds within an hour, compared to three months or longer for magazines (Britten, 2007). Professional fashion journalists also create popular blogs giving instant commentary on runway shows and revealing insights on their lives as industry insiders ("Defining moments," 2007).

The combination of high visibility and a very desirable status marker leads to speedy diffusion. The trend ends when the fashion has moved from group to group until almost anyone who wants the product has the product or a knockoff. In today's fast-paced marketplace, change becomes a constant. Celebrities, once famous, are eclipsed or replaced just as new status markers replace the original and begin trickling down.

The environment is a complex one, but the trickle-down theory of fashion change helps the forecaster visualize the interactions. By tracking the new fashionable elite, feeder groups for fashion ideas, and aggressively imitative groups, the forecaster becomes sensitized to the ways fashion trickles down in today's marketplace.

TRICKLE-ACROSS THEORY

Imagine a fashion observer in the early 1960s. How would they explain the fashion dynamics of the time? Nearly every characteristic of *la Belle Époque* had changed. Women gained the vote in 1920 and now have more access to education and the world of work than ever before. The United States fought two world wars, weathered the Great Depression of the late 1920s and throughout the 1930s, and fought to a standstill in the Korean conflict. In the early sixties, the United States is involved in a civil war in a far-off place called Vietnam. Civil rights and integration are social issues being dealt with in the courts and in the streets. Mass communication has come of age. Television is a potent influence on the behavior of American consumers. The great development era of department stores has ended, but the stores and other retail outlets have expanded the fashion market. Mass production has matured and provides fashion apparel at all price points.

For the first few years of the 1960s, the trickle-down theory of fashion change seemed as relevant as ever. John F. Kennedy was in the White House and his wife, Jacqueline, born into the affluent upper class, was an international style setter. Jacqueline Kennedy wore clothing from American and European designers and her hairstyles, clothing, and accessories were widely copied by American women in all classes. With President Kennedy's assassination in late November of 1963, that era came to an end. Jacqueline Kennedy would continue to be a style setter, but not on the same scale as during those early White House years.

Looking backward at the previous decades, a fashion observer would remember that fashion in the 1920s through the 1950s had an authoritarian flavor—one or two looks were considered fashionable and all other looks were

not. In the late 1950s, the youth culture began to be felt and the teenager had been discovered as a market segment. With the baby boom generation in its teen years, there was a shift away from traditional forms and establishment dictates. The original form of the trickle-down theory of fashion change did not provide sufficient explanations for the fashions of the 1960s. King (1963) said so in an article titled "A Rebuttal to the 'Trickle Down' Theory." He argued that society had changed in profound ways including:

- The "leveling influences" that had changed the profile of the consumer market.
- The accelerating spread of fashion awareness brought on by mass media.
- The accelerated transitions from season to season, resulting in almost nonexistent time lags such as those required for imitation and differentiation under the trickle-down theory.

King contended that the trickle-down theory of fashion change did not help the sophisticated marketer understand fashion behavior in the 1960s. Instead, he proposed a rival theory, the **trickle-across theory** of fashion change (also called the **mass market** or **simultaneous adoption theory**). Simply stated, the theory holds that fashion information trickles across horizontally

● ● ● activity 3.1. Group Identity

Identify a group that embodies the definitions of a new, visible elite or a fast-moving social group with a penchant for differentiation or an aggressively imitative group. Use visuals and descriptive words to describe the group's current look. What consumer segments are most likely to imitate the group's taste? Use the visualization of the trickle-down theory of fashion change to predict the next stages of fashion change. Prepare a presentation to communicate your prediction.

Figure 3.2.
The trickle-across theory of fashion change.

DIRECTION Horizontal across strata

TEMPO/SPEED Rapid and simultaneous

MASS MEDIA

DYNAMICS FASHION IDEAS ALL MARKET LEVELS

SOURCE OF FASHION IDEAS Couture with selection by professional gatekeepers

SOURCE OF CHANGE Innovators and influentials in each market strata

within social strata rather than vertically *across* strata (Figure 3.2). According to King, within a given fashion season, consumers in all socioeconomic groups simultaneously have the freedom to select from a range of styles, and this range is sufficient to satisfy personal taste. Rather than an elite introducing fashion ideas into society, King saw leadership within each social stratum and within each social group. In this view, personal influence plays the key role in the transmission of fashion information and two kinds of consumers are influential in popularizing new looks:

- The innovators—people who buy early, the earliest visual communicators of a season's styles.
- The influentials—those who are frequently asked for advice and define appropriate standards within their interpersonal networks.

Three factors were essential for the emergence of a mass market—mass production, mass communication, and a growing middle class. Mass communication—in the form of magazines, newspapers, television, and movies—made style information available to all simultaneously. Mass production made more looks available in any given season, offering the possibility of individual selection from among the many resources. Imitation and differentiation were still part of the dynamic because others would imitate innovators and influentials within their social strata and those fashion leaders would move to new looks.

Just as in the trickle-down theory of fashion change, designers play an important creative role. However, the gatekeepers had changed. Gatekeepers filter the many ideas proposed by designers and determine which will be disseminated widely and which will be discarded. In the trickle-down theory of fashion change, the gatekeepers were the fashionable and affluent elite who could afford the time and effort to view and select from the designers' collections. With mass media and mass production, a new set of gatekeepers rose to prominence—journalists, manufacturers, and

retailers. The professional gatekeeper's job was to view the designers' collections and select the styles to be featured in the media and produced in mass quantities (Figure 3.3).

The efficiency of mass production now enabled fashion ideas to be "knocked off" at all market levels within the same season, but that was not a new idea. In 1931, *Life* magazine reported on copies of the "Wally" dress, the $250 Mainbocher wedding ensemble worn by Mrs. Wallis Warfield Simpson when she married the Duke of Windsor (Figure 3.4). The dress appeared as a sketch in *Women's Wear Daily* on May 26 and by June 13 was available in the upscale Bonwit Teller store on New York's Fifth Avenue for $25. By early July it was featured in the window of a more moderately priced

department store for $16.95. One week later, it was on the racks of a cash-and-carry store for $8.90 ("The descent," 1931).

By 1960, the **knockoff** had become the normal way to do business in the fashion industry. The practice began in earnest after World War II when discounters like Ohrbach's purchased couture fashions at a prearranged price and made line-for-line copies in the exact fabric, even advertising them with the name of the original couture house. The practice of copying became an entrenched convention within the industry. Communication and production technology continued to speed up the process until by the 1990s, manufacturers could preempt designers by making a sample of a dress shown on the runway overnight and

Figure 3.3.
The press and buyers are the gatekeepers in a mass-production fashion system because they decide which looks are made available to the public at all price points. (*WWD*, Courtesy of Fairchild Publications)

deliver it to the stores ten days later, a feat that the designers could not duplicate (Betts, 1994). Under these conditions, the trickle-across theory seems the ideal explanation of fashion change.

Criticism of the Theory

One tenet of the trickle-across theory is that the interlocking technologies of mass communication and mass production speeded up the process so much that time lags between introduction at the highest price points and availability at the lower price points practically disappeared. But is that how the process actually plays out?

Behling (1985/1986) agrees with King that design piracy or knockoffs play an important part in today's fashion system. But she disagrees that this process occurs with the speed suggested by King's theory, which depends on fashion looks being simultaneously available at all levels of the marketplace. Instead, she identifies a time lag of at least a year between the point when

Figure 3.4.
The "Wally" dress, a $250 Mainbocher design worn by the Duchess of Windsor at her wedding, was quickly knocked off at lower price points.

the style has been identified through a trickle-down process, is manufactured and stocked by the retailer, and when it becomes available for purchase by the majority of consumers.

Behling attributes some of this time lag to the unwillingness of consumers at all levels to adopt the new look. What may seem the inevitable next step in fashion change to fashion insiders may not be accepted readily in another social setting. It often takes time for the consumer to build a comfort level with a proposed fashion, taking into account the mores of a particular locality or social group. For example, models who wore actual lingerie slips as dresses introduced the slip dress of 1994. Picked up by designers as a trend, it traveled from the runways to the editorial pages of fashion magazines to stores and to the more avant-garde consumers (Betts, 1994). But it continued to appear on the runways for several years as acceptance of the look grew across consumer segments. Behling was making her points before the time of fast-fashion stores like Zara, H&M, Forever 21, Mango, and Mexx. These chains offer of-the-moment trends, runway-inspired styles, and prices that make clothing disposable when the trend passes (Wilson, 2003). The fast-fashion chains are much nearer the ideal envisioned in the trickle-across theory because of their speed to market, rapid turnover of merchandise, and masterful use of mass communications and mass-production techniques.

Although it is undeniable that mass communication and mass production speeded up the process of moving fashion ideas from the runway to the store, Behling rightly points out exceptions to the functioning of the theory. Fashion change does not depend merely on mechanical and technological expertise. The speed of fashion change is regulated by the willingness of people to accept that change in numbers sufficient to make it profitable.

Forecaster's Toolbox: Theory in Action

The trickle-across theory of fashion change operates in an environment where designers propose fashion and gatekeepers such as journalists, manufacturers, and retailers determine which looks are reproduced in quantity at all price points. By providing a wide variety of looks at all price points simultaneously, the industry provides customers with the means to differentiate themselves from others through individual selection and the means to demonstrate group membership. Although the fashionable elite are still influential through mass communication, the key element in acceptance of a new look lies within the personal network and through the influence of innovators and influentials.

The real predictive power in a theory derives from its ability to clearly establish the source, the mechanism, the tempo, and the direction of fashion change. As in the trickle-down theory, the trickle-across theory of fashion change provides the fashion forecaster with the tools of the trade—an early warning system for identifying the next new thing and a paradigm for mapping out the direction and speed of the fashion change. The early warning system involves monitoring the interaction of designers' introductions of fashion ideas; the response of journalists, manufacturers, and retailers; and the acceptance or rejection reaction of consumers in different market segments. By being sensitive to the time lag inherent in the consumer acceptance of a new fashion, the fashion forecaster can predict when different market segments are most likely to move from awareness of a proposed fashion to interest in that fashion, to trying the look on, to purchase (and repurchase).

TRICKLE-UP THEORY

Imagine a fashion observer in the late 1960s. How would they explain fashion change? This time the focus is not on the apparel industry as in the trickle-across theory, but on a new source of inspiration and fashion leadership. Youthquake is under way on both sides of the Atlantic as young people discover the expressive qualities of fashion. The symbol of the decade—the miniskirt—emerges at the midpoint of the 1960s. It is a time when music, art, television variety shows, and movies all move to the youthful beat. The Beatles—John, Paul, George, and Ringo—revolutionize music, men's fashion, and the movies, along with the scruffier Rolling Stones. A new youthful

● ● ● activity 3.2. Who Are the Gatekeepers?

Learn the names and affiliations of the fashion executives who attend and the fashion press who report on the fashion shows. Each has an individual take on the world of fashion. These fashion insiders decide what looks are selected from the designers' collection to be disseminated more widely. Find out who they are by reading trade papers for reports on seasonal fashion shows. Collect clippings that feature quotes from these insiders describing their opinions. Some fashion journalists have blogs where they comment on what they are seeing and what is happening in up-to-the-minute detail. Watch fashion on television. Who is interviewed? What point of view do they represent? Read the editor's letter in the front of fashion magazines for insight on how the press covers fashion. Develop an insider's map of the world of fashion and know the names and positions of the key players.

Figure 3.5.
The trickle-up theory
of fashion change.

DIRECTION   Status markers trickle up from consumer stylists and subcultural groups

TEMPO/SPEED   Depends on the sensitivity of fashion gatekeepers and visibility of the subcultural groups

DYNAMICS

SOURCE OF FASHION IDEAS   Aesthetic codes of subcultural groups

SOURCE OF CHANGE   Instabilities in age, gender, ethnicity, and appearance

sensibility emerges and is expressed in the hippie and the flower child looks. Women become more militant in their demands for equality and express their frustrations with social restrictions by burning bras and demonstrating in the streets. Long hair, bare feet, and nudity become socially acceptable. Unisex and ethnic looks are highly valued badges of changing attitudes. Adults, the former arbiters of fashion, now take their fashion cues from the young.

Against this backdrop, Field (1970) proposed a new theory of fashion change he called the **status float phenomenon** (now commonly known as the **trickle-up theory** of fashion change). According to this theory, higher-status segments with more power imitated those with lower status—that is, status markers were floating up the status pyramid rather than trickling down or across it (Figure 3.5). To support this view, Field cited specific examples

from the culture. Some of his examples sound quaint and condescending today but were relevant and groundbreaking at the time.

- Black is beautiful—"Negro" music and dance had a strong influence on popular culture, as did "Negro" speech on American slang. In relationship to fashion, Field pointed out the increasing use of "Negro" models, actors, and celebrities on television, in magazines and advertising, and as spokespersons for products aimed at a broad audience. "Afro prints" in fabrics were featured in fashion magazine editorial pages. The popularity of hairstyles associated with African Americans could be seen in the wigs that allowed anyone in society to emulate the styles. Field suggests that the channels of jazz and youth culture moved "Negro" fashion into the consciousness of a wider audience.

- Youth culture—According to Field, extremes in fashion originally adopted by youth to express their rebellion against the older generation were adopted and worn by the middle-aged. In a specific example, he cited the case of formerly ultraconservative automotive executives who were "sporting sideburns, square-toed buckled shoes, short, cuffless pants, wide, flashy polka-dot ties, sport coats, colored shirts, and even sport shirts" by 1969. Field suggested that these executives were wearing fashions pioneered by the teenage and college-aged crowd.
- Blue-collar influence on white-collar consumers—Field saw the camping craze and the buying of pickup trucks by middle-class consumers as a case of typically blue-collar pursuits trickling up the status pyramid. Additionally he cited the use of garish male clothing and bright colors on automobiles as a shift from the conservative tastes of the upper class to the tastes of the lower class. He cited the adapting of work clothes—jackets, jeans, boots, and the sleeveless undershirt—into more widely popular casual clothing styles for men as another case of status float.
- **The Sexual Revolution**—Women had freely borrowed from men's fashion at least since Coco Chanel popularized the look in the 1920s. Field cites a reverse case of borrowing: by 1969, college men and entertainers had adopted flare pants, a style originally worn by women earlier in the decade.
- Style leadership by prostitutes—Field cited the high heel, the use of rouge and lipstick, and women smoking cigarettes as examples of customs that originated in the subculture of prostitutes and spread over the decades to middle- and upper-class women.

- Field concluded his article with a call for more research to document the extent of the status float phenomenon and its variations.

The trickle-up theory provides the cornerstone of today's view that street fashion is a laboratory for fashion change. The concept carries with it the essence of outsider sensibility. Simmel (1904) was aware of the connection between prostitutes and fashion except that he used the more refined term "demimonde" to refer to these fashion pioneers. He pointed out that an uprooted existence outside the bounds of acceptable society produced a "latent hatred against everything that has the sanctions of law" and that this hatred found expression in striving for new forms of appearance. It is this context of being dressed up, hanging out, and oozing attitude that finds expression in clothes, hairstyles, makeup, tattoos, body piercing, and accessories.

Today's fashion world takes the importance of street fashion for granted. Again, the motivation for differentiation drives **subcultures** where new looks are created. Members of these subcultures adopt specific aesthetic codes that differentiate them from other subcultures and from the mainstream (Blumberg, 1975). Imitation may occur between social groups but the importance of street fashion for the fashion industry is in the visual inspiration it provides for designers and other fashion gatekeepers such as journalists, stylists, and photographers.

Saint Laurent has been credited with reversing fashion's directional flow (Betts, 1994). He showed street-inspired trends on the runways as early as his 1960 collection for Dior. Later in the 1960s he was inspired

Figure 3.6.
Seattle-based organic garment supplier Greensource sells to clients such as Macy's, Inc. and Wal-Mart Stores, Inc. (*WWD,* Courtesy of Fairchild Publications)

by New York's army-surplus shops and by Paris student protesters. It did not take other designers long to catch onto street fashion, the youthful club scene, **vintage fashion**, and flea market finds as the source for fashion change. Inspired originally by the surf-oriented lifestyle, today's streetwear looks to disc jockeys, skateboarders, artists, and musicians for trends with context, affiliation, and meaning. Authentic streetwear is restricted to those with contacts and is acquired specifically for "the thrill of standing out and being different," but when the looks reach chain stores and become part of mainstream culture they "lose the feel" for the original audience (Pallay, 2007) (Figure 3.6).

In his book *Streetstyle: From Sidewalk to Catwalk,* Polhemus (1994) traces the appeal of street-inspired fashion to the quest for authenticity.

It represents hanging out on the wrong side of the tracks with "nohopers [who] have none of those things that our society officially decrees to be important (money, prestige, success, fame)" and yet represent something real and genuine. Polhemus sees street-style garments as radiating the power of their associations. He traces the chain of events, beginning with a genuine street-style innovation that is picked up and popularized through music, through dissemination to street kids in other locales, until it finds its way into an upscale version in a designer's collection. He calls the process **bubble up,** the opposite of trickle-down fashion. The groups whose fashions are appropriated may react in an unexpected way: they may be insulted rather than flattered because the appropriation waters down the significance of the objects, robbing them of their power and magic as symbols of differentiation.

Forecaster's Toolbox: Today in Action

Forecasters applying the trickle-up theory of fashion change (Field calls it status float and Polhemus, bubble up) look to **consumer stylists** as the source of creativity, as naïve designers who propose new looks. Such people are not waiting on every street corner. Two sources serve as early warning signs for trickle-up fashion—the alternative fashion neighborhoods and the fashion scouts.

Fashion Neighborhoods

A conduit from street culture to the fashion system exists in almost all large cities—a neighborhood where young outsiders come to hang out, shop, and keep up with each other. The entrepreneurs and retailers who set up shop in these areas are the first to pick up on new trends because, in many cases,

they participate directly in the social life and street culture their stores service. Often these colorful neighborhoods are a bit run-down and seedy, but they serve as a playground for free-spirited experimentation in lifestyles and dress. For the fashion forecaster, these neighborhoods offer the chance to see consumer stylists at work inventing the next new fashion (Figure 3.7).

Finding emerging trends means mounting an expedition to neighborhoods where young people congregate with the aim of observing people with unconventional style of dress. One student of the supertrendy Tokyo fashion scene in the Shibuya area spent more than a year walking the streets, taking pictures of the most fashionable people, and talking to them about fashion to increase her expertise. She even worked in a boutique to

Figure 3.7.

In the 1960s, London's Carnaby Street drew crowds of young people looking for mod styles and miniskirts. But it fell off fashion's radar. Its revival as a destination for trendsetting denim buyers depends on a mix of international brands, boutiques, and chic cafes. (*WWD*, Courtesy of Fairchild Publications)

sharpen her eye for what was truly stylish (Greenberg, 2007).

Fashion neighborhoods have shifting boundaries and a life cycle of their own. When established by boutiques and independent retailers, such areas become a target for fashion chains and designer stores. The Meatpacking District in New York was pioneered by boutiques that were replaced by luxury brands when their leases were up and owners couldn't pay the higher rent (Edelson, 2008). Chinatown replaced the Meatpacking district as "a very underground, indie thing"—an area for style seekers where fashion boutiques moved into affordable spaces scattered through the area (La Ferla, 2008c). In Los Angeles major companies are buying out leases in the destination shopping streets of Melrose Place and Robertson Boulevard. Meanwhile the independent retailers are staking out new areas on La Brea Avenue and Melrose Avenue (Vesilind, 2007). Fashion forecasters find these neighborhoods good locations for scouting new trends in merchandise and observing the fashion-forward shoppers.

● ● ● activity 3.3. Scouting for Change

Watch the fashion news for reports on fashion neighborhoods and subcultures feeding new looks into the fashion system. Use Internet search engines to locate newspaper and magazine articles by cultural journalists, bloggers, or fashion writers reporting on avant-garde social behavior and radical lifestyles. When a source describes a look or uniform associated with the behavior or lifestyle, estimate the path and time lag for these edgy looks to be transmitted into the fashion system. What consumer group is most likely to first adopt this trend? (Warning: Avant-garde, radical, and edgy all signify cultural behavior beyond the boundaries of mainstream. To many people, the ideas, behavior, and dress of such groups can be shocking. Do not assume the role of scout on the cultural edge unless you can be an objective, detached observer.)

Fashion Scouts

Because forecasters cannot watch the globally diverse subcultures that may be the origin of an emerging fashion look, they must rely on scouting reports from other professionals. The cues may come from the creative director for a fashion-forward retailer, the pages of an avant-garde publication, the windows of a shop on the side street of a fashion center, the reports of a forecasting service, or the articles of a cultural journalist. These scouts patrol the edges of culture, recognizing the potential and power of a subcultural style and transmitting it into the fashion system.

Another scouting opportunity exists in cyberspace with fashion blogs. Worldwide, there are about 800 fashion blogs written by citizen journalists or "prosumers" (professional consumers). Fashion blogs focus on a domain—street fashion relaying sightings almost instantly to readers, a particular category like status bags, celebrity shopping venues, personal fashion quests, or criticism (the fashion police) (Britten, 2007). The problem for forecasters is finding the relevant blogs using traditional search engines. Google takes as long as three weeks to index the Web and orders results by popularity. Blogs update daily and may be important for a small but important community of readers. However, new search engines specific to finding blogs index the Web daily and order results by most recent posts (Crow, 2007).

The Web offers another fresh and immediate source of fashion information— **social networking sites**. At general social networking sites like Facebook and MySpace the main activity is connecting to friends. But MySpace started a fashion page for "people who have any sort of interest in fashion, from small to large" and quickly created a community of "friends" (profiles). The site highlights the pages of stylish members, features emerging designers, and includes an *In Style* magazine news feed. Fashion-specific social networking sites like Iqons—a London-based site with connections to the fashion world in Europe—attract people who work in the industry (Corcoran, 2007d). Forecasters can stay close to the action by visiting social networking sites where people with an interest in fashion—consumers and professionals—meet to exchange information.

Applying the Theory in Today's Marketplace

The real predictive power in a theory derives from its ability to clearly establish the source, the mechanism, the tempo, and the direction of fashion change. As with the trickle-down and trickle-across theories, the concept of time lag plays an important part in the dynamics of fashion as it trickles up from the street corner Main Street. Looks developed as aesthetic codes for members of subcultural groups are usually too radical to be accepted instantly into mainstream fashion. It takes time for consumers' sensibilities to adjust to the proposed look and incorporate it into their own social setting. This time lag may be as short as a year or as long as several decades. The forecaster can estimate the path and time sequence by evaluating the degree of adjustment required, the visibility of the innovation to consumer segments, and the match between the symbolism of the look and the attitudes of the target consumers.

DIRECTIONAL THEORIES OF FASHION CHANGE IN TANDEM

A careful reading of the fashion theories reveals the interplay between the directional theories of fashion change. Simmel's article from 1904 contained the seeds not only of the trickle-down theory but pointed to the trickle-up theory through references to the conspicuously antifashion consumer and the demimonde as a source for fashion innovation. The instabilities of gender, ethnicity, age, and physical attractiveness that serve to update the trickle-down theory play an important part in the fashion statements of subcultural groups. A fashion forecaster's toolbox must come equipped with an understanding of how each theory represents a view of reality. But that is not enough. In a complex social system, it may take more than one theory to explain how a particular fashion moves from a starting point to widespread acceptance in everyday life.

A Model for Vertical Flow

Behling (1985/1986) saw common underlying themes in the two vertical theories of fashion—trickle down and trickle up—and sought to integrate them into a single predictive model. The model attempts to explain fashion change between 1920 and 1985 using the median age of the population and the economic health of the country as factors. When she arrays the decades on the horizontal axis and median age of the population in years on the vertical axis, a regular pattern appears. During time periods when the median age was low—the 1920s, and the mid-1960s to mid-1970s—fashion looks trickled up from youthful consumers to the market as a whole. During time periods when the median age was higher, fashion tended to trickle down from the older, wealthy, and influential strata.

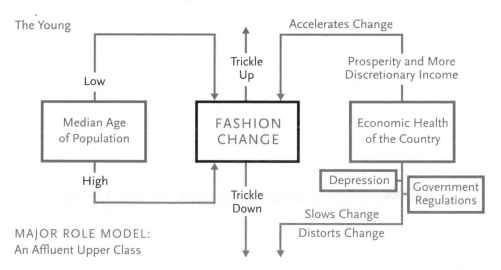

Figure 3.8.
The direction of fashion changes depends on several factors: the median age of the population, the economic health of the country, and the presence or absence of government regulation.

Behling's model shows a relationship between the median age of the population, fashion role models, and the direction of fashion flow. Events that can alter this directional flow are a depressed economy or curtailment of fashion by governmental decree, as in rationing (Figure 3.8).

Can this model can be applied to current demographic conditions? Because the median age is expected to rise as baby boomers enter middle age, the model suggests that fashion influence

should trickle down from an older, affluent, and visible class. Median age may be irrelevant in the late 2000s. The aging baby boomers—about 80 million consumers between 45 and 65 years old with high discretionary incomes—are matched by the millennials (also known as Gen Y)—62 million consumers from mid-teens to 30 years old with buying power and eager for the trendy styles, though still price conscious (Tran, 2008d). For a while, fashion marketers will have to pick their targets and watch for fashion change both down from the affluent and up from the street. But older consumers are less interested in fashion than younger consumers and, as the boomers leave the equation, median age may again be an indicator of fashion direction.

Time Lags and Idea Chains

The concept of time lags, apparent in each of the directional theories of fashion change, is an important issue in fashion forecasting. The technologies of mass communication and mass production that make possible the simultaneous adoption of a fashion across all market segments do not ensure such an outcome. Instead, the process often includes a time lag during which

● ● ● activity 3.4. **Idea Chains**

Select a fashion item—the T-shirt, denim jacket, stiletto heels, sneakers—and develop an idea chain. Show the origin of the item and trace its path into mainstream fashion. What celebrities, social movements, movies, music, or other cultural shifts were involved? Sources for this investigation include:

- Magazine articles on specific fashion items because they often include a brief history of how the item evolved.

- Books on the history of fashion in the twentieth century because they often integrate the evolution of particular looks into a more complex time line.

Find pictures to illustrate stages in the idea chain. Prepare a presentation as a visualization of your findings.

consumers become more aware, interested, and receptive to the new fashion—a trickle-down process. Street looks go through stages of modification that lead to wider acceptance.

Polhemus (1994) traces the path of the black leather motorcycle jacket from a functional beginning to a World War II designation of bravery and daring when worn by pilots, to a symbol of rebellious youth produced primarily by small, family-owned shops in off-Main Street locations in the late 1950s. Immortalized in the movie *The Wild One* by screen icon Marlon Brando, the jacket was still not acceptable in Main Street society. Only gradually did the black leather motorcycle jacket become normal everyday wear through the 1970s and 1980s. Helping the look gain in popularity was its adoption by visible fashionable elites—rock musicians from Jim Morrison to Bruce Springsteen to George Michael. Fashion-forward designers known for street-inspired fashion, such as Katharine Hamnett and Jean-Paul Gaultier, first introduced the look to the runway. Designers such as Claude Montana, Thierry Mugler, and Gianni Versace further appropriated it into high fashion. In the designer version, the look was then available to professional gatekeepers for dissemination through mass media and mass production.

In the history of this one style, all three directional theories of fashion change act at different stages. First the style moves from a street fashion for a particular subculture to diffusion among other outsider groups. Then it is adopted by the visible elite of rock musicians, appropriated by designers, and presented on the runway. Knockoffs make it available to all market segments. Mass communication aids its acceptance by mainstream consumers. At each stage there were opportunities for fashion forecasters to recognize and map the process. The evolution of the "antihero's anti-sports

coat" continues even when the original images—pilots, motorcycle gangs—are anachronistic. Today's softer version merges many stylistic characteristics to create a look that can be worn with jeans or with shirt and tie (Colman, 2008a).

In a 1992 *Newsweek* magazine cover story (Alter, 1992) on the cultural elite, an accompanying graphic introduced the concept of an **idea chain**—a set of linked events that move a phenomenon from a subculture to mainstream. The subject of the article's exercise was rap music. The chain began in 1968 when a West Bronx disc jockey invented hip-hop. The style was elaborated on during the 1970s with the addition of break dancing and the first small record labels specializing in this form of music. By 1981, the new wave band Blondie had a rap song as a No. 1 hit. During the mid- and late 1980s, collegiate rappers, corporate record companies such as Columbia, and MTV took rap to the middle-class consumer. The 1990 film *House Party* further popularized the hip-hop idiom, and the sitcom *Fresh Prince of Bel-Air* brought rap to weekly primetime television. No single event or influential celebrity or corporate sponsor was sufficient to move the idea along the chain. Instead, it took the entire chain of events played out over time.

In the same way, a single directional theory of fashion change is sufficient only to explain particular links in the chain, not the whole time line as an idea moves from source to wide public acceptance. A forecaster in New York tuned into the right radio station in the late 1960s may have recognized rap music as a trend and begun considering the marketing potential. But there were other sightings throughout the 1970s and 1980s that offered the same opportunity to participate in the full-blown mass acceptance of the style in the early 1990s. At every stage, there were marketing opportunities for the music and for the fashion looks associated with it.

Long-Wave Phenomenon and Fashion Cycles

Visualize the dynamics of fashion as waves striking a beach. Long before one wave has finished its course, new ones are being formed far out in the ocean. Each wave follows the others to shore, with an occasional large wave appearing between sets of smaller ones (Brenninkmeyer, 1973). Each wave rolling toward shore has a curve, a crest, and a crash (Collins, 1974). The comparison can be taken further to explain the wave forms:

> Some waves race headlong for a shallow beach, swell rapidly to a tremendous foaming top, then drop abruptly with a thud. Is this not precisely what happens with fads? But other waves move gradually upwards, curl over in a quiet, leisurely way, then break with little or no force. Is this not precisely the movement of sane, properly conceived style cycles? They are slow to develop, hold their own for a time, then subside rather than collapse. (p. 24)

Imagine a forecaster standing on the beach and watching the formation of fashion waves. How far out can he or she see? What are the size and shapes of waves coming toward the beach? What is the underlying contour of the bottom, and how does that influence the shape and speed of the waves? When will the waves arrive and with what force? If a forecaster can estimate these factors, then that gives a designer, manufacturer, or retailer a chance to capitalize on change. Part of that estimate involves recognizing **fashion cycles**—fashion ideas that return periodically to popularity.

RECYCLING FASHION IDEAS

Designers raid fashion's closet for inspiration, returning fashions from every decade to the runways. Recycling fashion ideas is part of **historic continuity**—the steady evolution of clothing including the continual recurrence of symbolism, styles, and elements of decoration (Brenninkmeyer, 1973). When some style is neglected for a period of time, it is ripe for revival. In the early 1980s an era of conservatism aligned with "preppy" fashion—an "old money" style borrowed from the New England prep school wardrobe of chinos and polo shirts, print dresses with ribbon belts, cardigans and madras blazers. The style revived in the mid-2000s in an era of uncertainty and war as nostalgia for better times and as a "buttoned up" response to a period when fashion showed a lot of skin (Jackson, 2005). Although never revived exactly in form or with the same companion elements, the style is recognizably retro (from the prefix meaning backward). **Retro fashion** carries with it the nostalgia for other periods when that look was the prevailing fashion (Figure 3.9). Several theories of fashion change deal with the recurring nature of fashion.

The Theory of Shifting Erogenous Zones

One of the key characteristics of eveningwear in the 1930s was the bare back look. Laver (1973) noticed these sexy dresses and compared them to short skirts in the previous decade, when the emphasis was on the legs. From this and other examples he suggested that fashion changed systematically by covering one part of the body while uncovering another. As he explained, parts of the female body, which are exposed by a fashion, lose their erotic power to attract over time. When this happens, the fashion goes out of style. Another part

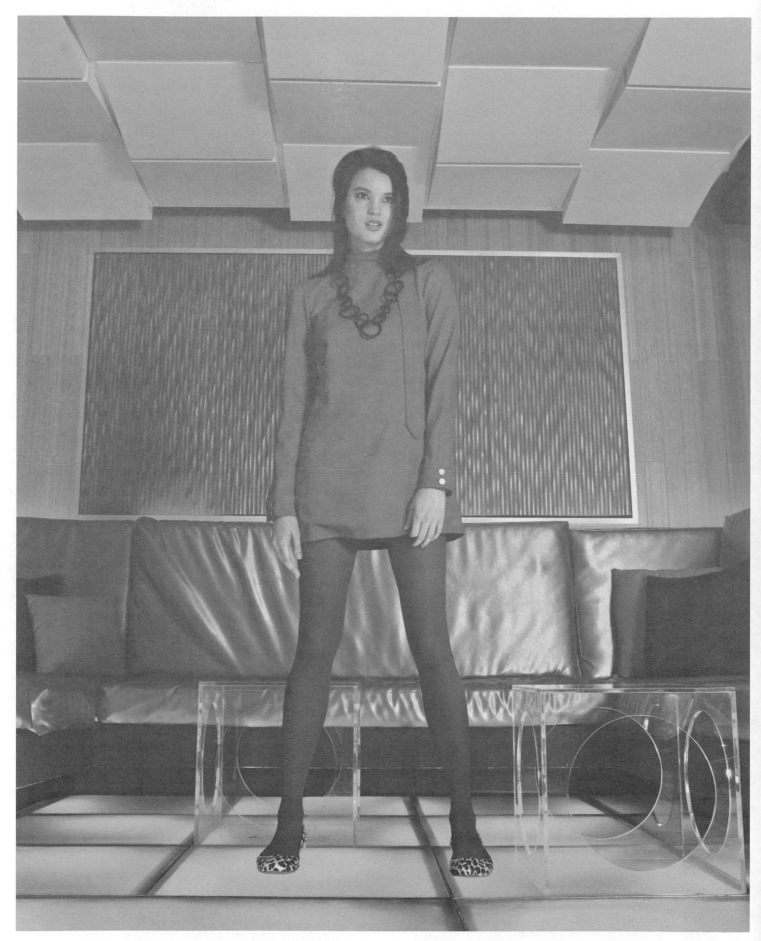

Figure 3.9.
Mod styles such as short minidresses recall the swinging sixties. Styles reminiscent of that time in fashion history recycle every few years, whenever the spirit of the times make people nostalgic for a more upbeat era.
(*WWD*, Courtesy of Fairchild Publications)

of the body, one that has been hidden or deemphasized during the previous period, becomes the focus of attention for the next fashion cycle. The newly emphasized part of the body becomes an **erogenous zone**. Any part of the female body may become the focus of erotic attention, and the erogenous zone is always shifting. Laver (1973, p. 383) said, "it is the business of fashion to pursue it, without ever catching up."

Other scholars (Wilson, 1985) disputed Laver's theory of shifting erogenous zones by saying that it applies only to female fashion, that his examples can be explained in other ways, and that the meaning of any apparel item is too complex for so easy an interpretation. Although Laver's theory may not offer a sufficient explanation of fashion cycles, it does point to an important element of newness that can be part of fashion trends. Fashion does play an important part in seduction and attracting sexual attention. Even in the use of cosmetics, the emphasis shifts—sometimes to the eyes, other times to the mouth or the cheeks. In the same way, different parts of the body are emphasized during different fashion eras.

In discussing the history of the bathing suit, historian Lena Lencek (1996) described changes in styles in terms of shifting erogenous zones. In the early part of the century, bathing suits were very concealing; the only uncovered parts of the body were the ankles and wrists. By the 1920s, the bathing suit was beginning to shrink in size, but the torso was still mostly covered, so the emphasis was on the legs and arms. Similar to the evening dresses of the 1930s, the swimsuits of that era put emphasis on the bare

back. New fabrics and bra technology made possible more structured suits in the 1940s and 1950s and the emphasis was on the bosom. When the bikini was introduced in the 1960s, emphasis shifted to the navel. Very revealing suits were seen on the beaches in Brazil and St. Tropez (in southern France) but arrived in other places with the fitness craze in the 1970s and 1980s. The new look emphasized a part of the body that had not previously been visible— the toned and muscled upper thighs and hip, which were revealed by high-cut swimsuits. For the daring in the 1990s, thong suits bared a new part of the female body, the derriere. The changes in swimsuit styling through the decades are reminiscent of Laver's theory of shifting erogenous zones.

Forecaster's Toolbox: Theory in Action

Although the theory of shifting erogenous zones may explain only a small percentage of fashion change, it is still a useful concept. The area above the breast—collarbones and upper chest—has rarely, if ever, been considered an erogenous zone until it became a badge of thinness. In a period when dresses covered as much as they revealed, prominent collarbones signified a thin body underneath and radiated an uncontroversial sex appeal (Jesella, 2007). Laver's theory helps explain the underlying mechanism that makes revealing or emphasizing one part of the body over all others seem new. It also explains how, after a time, the look no longer has the same effect. When this occurs, designers change the silhouette, the cut, the fit, the detail, and the emphasis to create a new fashion look.

Figure 3.10.
Rudy Gemreich's
1968 bikini illustrates
this era's shift in
emphasis to the navel.
(*WWD*, Courtesy of
Fairchild Publications)

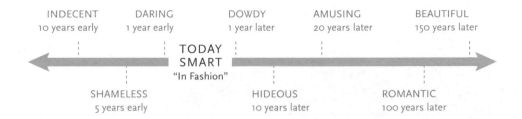

INDECENT
10 years early

DARING
1 year early

DOWDY
1 year later

AMUSING
20 years later

BEAUTIFUL
150 years later

TODAY
SMART
"In Fashion"

SHAMELESS
5 years early

HIDEOUS
10 years later

ROMANTIC
100 years later

Figure 3.11.
Laver's "gap in appreciation" can be visualized as the period during which old fashion looks are rehabilitated or consumers become comfortable with an innovative look.

RETRO AND VINTAGE FASHION

When people look back at fashions recently past, they find them at best amusing, at worst distasteful. As Laver (1973) put it:

> Most women . . . will give as their opinion that the fashions of yesterday were indeed ridiculous, and that the fashions of the present day are both beautiful and practical. Women were probably always of this opinion, and all that can be said about it is that it is a complete delusion. (p. 381)

Laver did more than just notice this trait; he established a time line of acceptability (Figure 3.11). Looking backward, fashions closest to the present he said look dowdy. He developed a stepwise rehabilitation of a look, from frumpy and ridiculous for recently past fashion to beautiful for fashion 150 years in the past. On a somewhat shorter time line, he suggested that innovative looks being introduced into the fashion mix were likely to be considered audacious and brazen. Only as they moved closer to full acceptance were they deemed appropriate attire. Laver called this trick of seeing current fashion as exemplary when compared to past and future fashions the "gap in appreciation" and suggested that it exists in all matters of taste.

As a style, look, or lifestyle moves further into the past, it becomes a candidate for revival because the perception of it changes. Fashion change is often the result of revising an obsolete style or reinventing an outdated trend.

Forecaster's Toolbox: Theory in Action

Laver's ideas about recycling fashion provide a time line that forecasters can use in gauging probable reactions to fashion revivals. But not everything gets revived. Hats, announced again and again as returning to the fashion picture, never became as ubiquitous as they were in the 1920s through the 1950s. Miuccia Prada, Ralph Lauren, Marc Jacobs, and Madonna (for H&M) all showed turbans and cloche styles in Spring 2007, at the same time the Fashion Institute of Technology exhibited the hats of Lilly Daché, a famous milliner of the 1950s. But it wasn't enough to overcome the old-fashioned stigma of hats (Wilson, 2007a). Whatever is selected for revival tends to be something nostalgic or a campy novelty or some guilty pleasure that is currently forbidden.

The 1950s were first revived in the early 1970s ("Back to the 50s," 1972), as Laver's time line predicts—about 20 years after the original and just enough time to be considered amusing. Not revived were the political upheavals, bomb tests, and civil rights issues that had plagued the decade. Instead the revival concentrated on the fun of hula hoops, rock and roll, early Elvis, and the return to classic looks in fashion. Bits and pieces of the 1950s continue to be revived. In their turn, the 1970s were revived in the 1990s. According to Laver's time line, this occurred when the fashions of the 1970s could be defined as amusing. At the end of the 1990s, it was possible to sample many eras from super-wide bell-bottoms reminiscent of the 1970s to clam-diggers and capri pants, signature looks of the late 1950s.

Prices at fashion auctions and secondhand shops echo Laver's idea of a gap in appreciation. Caroline Reynolds Milbank, a fashion historian and consultant to an auction house, says that prices depend on the age of the item (Browne, 1994): "It takes a while for people to get far enough away. Clothes from the '50s and '60s will sell for three to four thousand dollars. The '70s are at a tenth of these prices." Similar to the theory of erogenous zones, Laver's time line of acceptability explains only one aspect of fashion change, but even a partial explanation can represent potential profits for a forecaster and his or her clients.

Like the 1950s styles, some looks are constantly recycled. Menswear looks for women first made an appearance when Coco Chanel began borrowing tweeds from the closet of her aristocratic English lover. From the mid-1940s to mid-1950s (Figure 3.12), high school girls appropriated blazers, crewneck sweaters, Oxford shirts, and blue jeans from brothers and boyfriends as their casual uniform (Feitelberg, 1996). Diane Keaton's *Annie Hall* look of 1977 had the same borrowed-from-boys élan.

The 1990s saw waves of revivals of past fashion eras—revivals of the tailored suits of the 1940s, the club scene of the 1950s, the psychedelic 1960s, the bell-bottoms and platform shoes of the 1970s, and hints of the extravagant, colorful, affluent 1980s. In the early 2000s, "the vintage craze" was a force in fashion. Celebrities wearing vintage on the runways generated media coverage because vintage represented the ultimate in luxury given its rareness, and marked the star as an individualist and trendsetter (Jones, 2003) (Figure 3.13). A popular vintage resource is Doris Raymond, who

Figure 3.12.
High school girls from the mid-1940s to the mid-1950s appropriated looks from the closets of their brothers and boyfriends and made them their own.

Figure 3.13.
Selma Blair in
vintage Chanel.
(*WWD*, Courtesy of
Fairchild Publications)

●●● activity 3.5. Venture into Vintage

What fashion is poised for revival? What fashion from the latter half of the twentieth century will become collectible? Which designer's work or celebrity's clothing is likely to bring high prices in future fashion auctions? What effect does an interest in vintage fashion have on designer evolution? Explore these kinds of questions by:

- Shopping secondhand shops to analyze differences in prices between styles and decades.
- Visiting vintage clothing sites on the Web (see the Resource Pointers section at the end of the chapter).
- Visiting Web sites on retro lifestyles.
- Using database searches to locate articles on fashion auctions.

owns The Way We Wore on Los Angeles' La Brea Avenue—a popular destination for vintage-wearing actors. Her 4,000-square-foot, two-story store is merchandised according to current fashion dictates, but her huge inventory in the warehouse next door offers inspiration to designers such as Michael Kors, Zac Posen, and Tory Burch, as well as wardrobe solutions to costume designers for period movies and television (Medina, 2007). If the clothes themselves are not available, the fashion insiders buy vintage magazines (Trebay, 2001).

Not only women's wear but menswear looks to vintage. Two leading menswear firms were among the most prominent bidders at the auction of the Duke of Windsor's apparel (Vasilopoulos, 1998). Even the window of Marc Jacobs on Bleecker Street features an occasional treasure trove like vintage military coats from Copenhagen for a mere $59 (Colman, 2008c).

●●● activity 3.6. Pendulum Swings

Use five years of back issues of a fashion magazine to backcast the pendulum swings of fashion. To narrow the search, check only key issues for each year, the ones most likely to preview seasonal fashion. Look for a season where the fashion news was a tight fit; then look back further to locate a season when loose and unconstructed fashion was considered newsworthy. Or, look for a season featuring short skirts, and look back to a time when longer skirts or pants dominated the runways. Now look at the seasons in between the extremes, or consider the work of a particular designer over several years. Is there the same kind of shift in emphasis between extremes? This kind of analysis requires a kind of abstraction of a fashion message. In every season there will be some tight- and some loose-fitting styles, and some variation in hem length. For this activity, look for the overall message, theme, or newness expressed in the issue. Use the pendulum visualization to explain your findings.

Figure 3.14.
The pendulum swing of fashion can be visualized as moving from a point of exaggeration in one direction toward one in the opposite direction. The midpoint represents the classic form as a compromise between the two extremes.

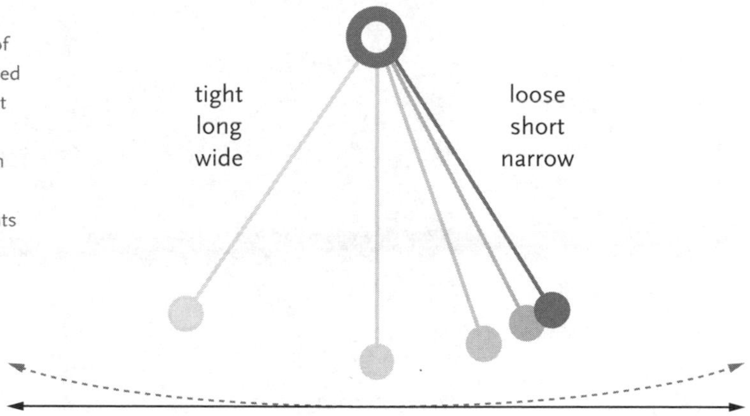

tight
long
wide

loose
short
narrow

THE PENDULUM OF FASHION

Just as a pendulum in a grandfather's clock swings back and forth keeping time, so the pendulum of fashion swings from a point of exaggeration and then moves in the opposite direction (Robinson, 1975). In this kind of fashion cycle, a trend terminates when all possibilities have been exhausted (Blumer, 1969). When short skirts get as short as possible, the pendulum swings toward longer skirts. When the fit gets too body conscious and cannot fit any tighter, the pendulum swings toward looser cuts. When black dominates the market for a time, brighter or lighter colors move in to relieve the gloom.

In an idealized version of this kind of cycle, a fashion look would evolve to a point of exaggeration in one direction, move toward the opposite direction, pause at the compromise point on a classic form, and then swing in the opposite direction (Figure 3.14). Such cycles can be traced in historic fashion (Young, 1937), but modern fashion tends to take a more abrupt path between extremes.

Hemline changes epitomize this kind of fashion cycle. The thigh-high miniskirt, which dates from about 1965, was new to fashion and lifted all skirts to the knee or just above it by

the early 1970s. Attempts to lower hemlines by the introduction of midi (mid-calf length) and maxi (floor length) were unsuccessful. But skirts did eventually come down. Change in the opposite direction marked 1989 when, after seasons of knee-length or below-knee-length skirts, designers reintroduced short skirts. The quick change alienated working women who refused to buy the garment. Retailers were left with stock to mark down and the press reported the short skirts as a failed trend. But skirt lengths did rise in the early 1990s, and the fashion-forward customer did wear miniskirts again and, eventually, microminis. By 1997, short skirts had gotten very short. Then designers found a way to go even shorter by adding slits. But by the fall of 1998, Kal Ruttenstein, senior vice president of fashion direction at Bloomingdale's, thought that short skirts looked stale. Runways for the Fall 1998 season showed floor-sweeping long looks (Schiro, 1998).

Whereas modern fashion does not follow the idealized pendulum swing between extreme points, the cycle does manifest itself in fashion change. The pendulum action can act on hemlines, fashion colors, looks, and even lifestyles. In 1995 IBM dropped its dark-suit dress code, introducing an era of casual clothing at the office. A survey by Levi Strauss showed that two years later, nine out of ten white-collar workers could take advantage of Casual Fridays, and about half could wear office casual all week (Loftus, 1999). By 2002, some corporations were reinstating business dress codes; a move was justified as a way to reassure clients in difficult economic times. Five years later, men had again embraced the striped dress shirt in oxford or broadcloth and tie, but the style was adapted—pared-down, button cuffs instead of French, a soft collar, and no breast pocket. The more edgy customer chose the Bengal stripe (classic $\frac{1}{8}$-inch wide) but with an extra-slim fit (Colman, 2008b). Dressing up looked new again (Figure 3.15).

David Wolfe, creative director for the fashion trend forecasting division of the Donegar Group, invoked the pendulum swing in a speech to the National Retail Federation (1998). Wolfe explained: "Think of fashion as moving slowly from sloppy casual to dressed up. It's going to take a long time. What's in the middle? What fills the gap? Classics are as comfortable as casual wear but they are a bit more traditional, tend to look a little more polished. They are halfway between casual and formal." The designer collections for Fall 2008 shifted from baby-doll dresses and miniskirts to sculptured feminine silhouettes, good tailoring, and sedate colors in the style of Grace Kelly or Jacqueline Kennedy. Even the bras and corsets women once burned were again on display along with satin-panel girdles—necessary undergarments for structured silhouettes. Some viewed the shift as a rebuke to the dishevelment of young Hollywood (La Ferla, 2008a). For fashion professionals and forecasters, the visualization of fashion's pendulum swing helps to define fashion direction and aids in predicting the next fashion change.

Figure 3.15.
Ties, once out, returned when young men discovered dressing up as a countertrend to casual for all occasions. (*WWD*, Courtesy of Fairchild Publications)

WAVE DYNAMICS

People look for patterns in everyday happenings such as the weather and the stock market. Why not look for cyclical patterns in fashion change? Is there an inner logic peculiar to fashion? Is some aspect of fashion immune to exogenous factors (external influences)? Is there a rhythm underlying the seemingly random fluctuations in fashion? Is there a discernible pattern that recurs over time? Researchers in the twentieth century searched for such a pattern (see Table 3.1). Such research tends to use similar methods:

Step 1   Find a suitable source for fashion images—fashion periodicals are frequently used.

Step 2   Because not all images can be included in the sample, develop a systematic way to decide which images will be excluded (e.g., images where the model is not pictured full length and facing forward).

Step 3   Standardize a set of measurements or observations to be taken on every image in the sample.

Step 4   Sample time as well as images by developing a systematic way to decide which issues of a periodical will be used and for what span of years (e.g., April and September issues from 1920 through 1990).

Step 5   Gather the data and analyze to reveal patterns of fashion change.

Researchers doing these rigorous **fashion counts** did find regularities and recurring patterns. Kroeber found evidence for a recurring pattern in skirt length of 35 years and skirt width every 100 years, 50 years for the pendulum swing from wide to narrow and 50 years for the swing back to wide. Young found a recurring pattern among back

fullness, tubular, and bell-shaped skirts, with steady evolution between the styles of 30 to 40 years. But these findings all apply to fashion before 1935.

The long-term cycles identified by Kroeber and Young and verified by other researchers are of little use to forecasters because the cultural institutions that created them no longer exist. Changes in women's status, the development of the automobile, and drastic shifts in culture terminated such cycles. Instead of slow evolution in styles, after 1935 there were increasing numbers of different styles available in the market at any given time (Belleau, 1987; Carman, 1966). More consumers became involved in being fashionable in their styles of life because of increasing levels of income, education, and leisure. With mass production, designers shifted from selling to individuals to selling to professional buyers representing large-scale retailers. Mass media increased coverage of the role of celebrities and their part in setting fashion. These cultural and industry changes meant that style options were more numerous and changed more frequently after 1935.

Still, researchers are fascinated by the idea of discovering evidence of long-term cyclical fashion change. Robinson (1975) was interested in economic cycles and saw potential in Kroeber's findings. He decided to do his own research to see if men were just as prone to following fashion as women. He analyzed the styles of men's whiskers—sideburns, sideburns with mustache, mustache alone, beard, and no facial hair—between 1842 and 1972. He found a wave of beard wearing started about the beginning of the study and disappeared around 1940. The mustache began a sharp rise in popularity in 1870 but bottomed out in 1970. He also found a long-term cyclical wave for men wearing some form of whiskers rising between 1842 and 1885 and declining until 1970. He also charted the

table 3.1. Research on Fashion Cycles

RESEARCHER	TIME PERIOD	FOCUS	FINDINGS
Kroeber (1919)	1844–1919	Width and length of women's evening dresses.	Skirt length recurred every 35 years. Skirt width recurred every 100 years, 50 years for the transition from wide to narrow and 50 years for the transition back again.
Richardson & Kroeber (1940)	1605–1936	Width and length of women's evening dresses.	Skirts alternate from broad to narrow, from long to short, with a regular cycle of 100 years.
Young (1937)	1760–1937	Style of skirts.	Cycle: back fullness to tubular to bell shape, each style ascending to dominance and evolving into the next cycle over 30 or 40 years.
Lowe & Lowe (1982, 1984, 1985)	1789–1980	Width and length of women's dresses.	Cycles expected to occur between 1937 and 1980 according to the Kroeber prediction did not occur. Instead there was increased variation within each year in terms of details of style.
Carman (1966)	1786–1965	Width and length of women's evening dresses.	Support for Young's identified cycles. Cyclical changes in waist and skirt dimensions. Periods when the cycles do not explain the changes observed—the decade of the 1860s, the decade of the 1920s, and from 1935 to 1966.
Weeden (1977)	1920–1976	Width and length of women's day dresses.	Data indicated the fashion process was speeding up and no style dominated a period.
Belleau (1987)	1860–1980	Women's day dresses: skirt length, waist emphasis, silhouette, fit of the sleeve, bodice, and skirt.	Cyclical movement in skirt length and waist emphasis. Cyclical characteristics in silhouette shapes—back fullness, tubular, bell, and hourglass. Beginning about 1935, more than one silhouette coexisted in the same period.
Lowe & Lowe (1990)	1789–1980	Width and length of women's evening dresses.	Failed to find accelerating change in fashion, but they did find evidence of increased rates of within-year variation.

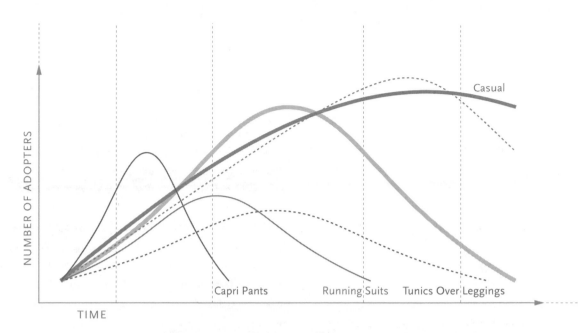

NUMBER OF ADOPTERS

Casual

Capri Pants   Running Suits   Tunics Over Leggings

TIME

Figure 3.16.
The long-wave change toward casual attire is made up of many other trends of shorter duration and different levels of acceptance.

swings in automobile styles between 1927 and 1974. He found that inch by inch the car roof had come down, necessitating numerous and costly redesigning as if "fashion were a heavy hammer, pounding the car body ever flatter" (p. 125). He concluded that there is a master force that he called "the style of life" that acts like Adam Smith's "invisible hand" in economics to guide fashion change. He concluded that long-term fashion cycles involve so many years that they are outside the influence of external events such as wars, technological innovation, and economics shifts.

The search for long-wave cycles in fashion change is fueled by the desire to improve the accuracy in predictions. The idea is that just as long-term trends in lifestyles exist, so does an underlying logic in fashion evolution. In this view, seasonal fluctuations are the visible short-run phenomenon that move fashion along from a precursor style to the current look, and beyond. But these jumps and starts are part of a larger wave of change (Figure 3.16). With new computer technology, improved research facilities, and new methods, it may be possible for researchers today to carry on this line of research. Computer software now exists to search large databases of numbers for patterns that are not discernible to humans. Perhaps these new research tools hold the opportunity to study the

multiplicity of looks after 1935 and discover more evidence of long-term cycles in fashion.

Forecaster's Toolbox: Theory in Action
Robinson's master force, style of life, can be a useful concept for product planners who need to forecast long-range change. He advised them to seek revelations among the most outrageous minority forms of conventional taste. These harbingers of change should be taken seriously when a few thousand consumers have bought into the form. Both the long- and short-term prognosticator should consider not only what the professionals are doing but also what the amateurs in a field are doing. The amateurs, enthusiasts, hobbyists, and buffs are often a compass for coming fashions in terms of dress and home decor. Producers no longer dictate fashion direction and consumers themselves often point the way to the next big thing, but only if a product planner is attuned to the signal. Finally, Robinson suggested that even the long fashion cycles are bounded by extremes, and a 50-year design shift is accomplished with an average yearly adjustment of 2 percent. This small incremental change gives the product planner a chance to decide what the consumer will want next year and ten years from then.

Key Terms and Concepts

Androgyny

Bubble up

Chase and flight

Conspicuous consumption

Conspicuous counter-consumption

Conspicuous leisure

Consumer stylists

Erogenous zone

Fashion blogs

Fashion counts

Fashion cycles

Gender bending

Gender blending

Historic continuity

Idea chain

Knockoff

Mass-market theory

Retro fashion

Reverse ostentation

Simultaneous adoption theory

Social networking sites

Status float phenomenon

Status markers

Subcultures

Trickle-across theory

Trickle-down theory

Trickle-up theory

Vintage fashion

Discussion Questions

Direction of Fashion Change

How does the trickle-down theory explain fashion movement today? Who are the visible fashionable elite today? Who are the people who exercise fashion leadership through their ability to use fashion artistically to create a style? How does the trickle-across theory explain fashion movement today? What happens to fashion in the long run if the knockoff is the usual way of doing business? How does the trickle-up theory explain fashion movement today? Do the sources for trends today parallel those identified by Field in 1970? Why are there time lags in fashion change?

Fashion cycles: What two frameworks deal with recycling fashion ideas? What is the difference between the pendulum effect of fashion in the first part of the twentieth century and the latter half? How can long-term cycles act like an "invisible hand," guiding fashion change? How useful are long-term cycles to a fashion forecaster?

Additional Forecasting Activities

Conspicuous Examples. Make a visual dictionary of examples of (1) conspicuous leisure, (2) conspicuous consumption, and (3) reverse ostentation or conspicuous counterconsumption. Use as a time line the entire twentieth century or one decade. How will they be expressed in the future? Will one be more dominant than the others?

Classic Compromises. Study classics like the blazer, pleated skirts, trousers, five-pocket jeans, and the sheath dress as representations of midpoint compromises in the fashion pendulum. Using the fashion pendulum visualization, illustrate the extreme versions of the style. Analyze the cycle length between fashion extremes and the classic midpoint. Predict the future of these classic styles. Will they continue basically unchanged?

What elaboration and details are likely to be grafted onto these classics to create the perception of newness?

Taste in Transition. Find pictures of fashion looks along Laver's time line of acceptability. Make a flash card of each look—the characteristic look from 5 years ago, from 20 years ago, and so on. Then find pictures of fashion-forward styles, and make flash cards of each. Use the flash cards to test Laver's theory. Show the cards in random order to people who vary in age, income, and clothing preferences. Ask each person to look at the cards and then choose an adjective from Laver's list to describe the styles. Write down the descriptors used for each card. Does your research agree or disagree with Laver's theory?

Resource Pointers

Vintage clothing sites on the Web, many with links to other sites, including those that deal with retro lifestyles:

    www.ballyhoovintage.com
    www.vintagevixen.com
    www.fashiondig.com
    www.poshgirlvintage.com
    www.coutureallurevintage.com

The couturier
does not create
fashion, he
interprets it.
—Yves Saint Laurent

7
THE LOOK: DESIGN CONCEPTS AND STYLE DIRECTIONS

OBJECTIVES
- Understand the evolution of today's information environment.
- Examine the concept of style tribes as an organizing principle.
- Appreciate the skills and abilities required of forecasters.
- Understand the fashion calendar and the interactions that create directional information.
- Develop skills in identifying trends, analyzing visual and symbolic core concepts, and synthesizing directional information for clients.
- Develop skills in research trends.

Trend Multiplication

In his book *The Empire of Fashion*, Lipovetsky (1994) identified three modern eras in fashion. The first began in the 1860s when the first couturier, Charles Frederick Worth, set up a fashion house in Paris, began showing designs prepared in advance, changed styles frequently, and employed models to show the clothes to clients. The second began in the 1960s with the ready-to-wear revolution. While the earlier system continued, mass production and mass media reconfigured the structure. With the rise of mass production and mass media, being "in fashion" became possible and desirable for more and more people (Figure 7.1). The third era, beginning in the late 1980s, was characterized by:

- Extreme diversity from one designer to another.
- The proliferation in the number of acceptable looks.
- Increased autonomy among consumers.
- A feminist movement that promoted functional, less restrictive, and more comfortable apparel.
- The disappearance of clear-cut differences between what was outdated and in fashion.

The dating of the three eras is arbitrary. The system in each era survived into the succeeding era and the seeds of the new era already existed in the old. Still, Lipovetsky's divisions are a convenient way to view change. Organizing observations into a time line and characterizing each segment allows the observer to see the shape of change, and the antecedents and consequences of change become more apparent.

THE FIRST ERA OF MODERN FASHION

During the first 100 years of modern fashion (from the 1860s to the 1960s), Paris was known as the center of innovation and set the annual trends followed by the rest of the world. Organized fashion shows on fixed dates began after World War I, an innovation that coincided with France's need for fashion as an export and the influx of professional buyers from the United States and other countries in Europe. The professional buyers, through a

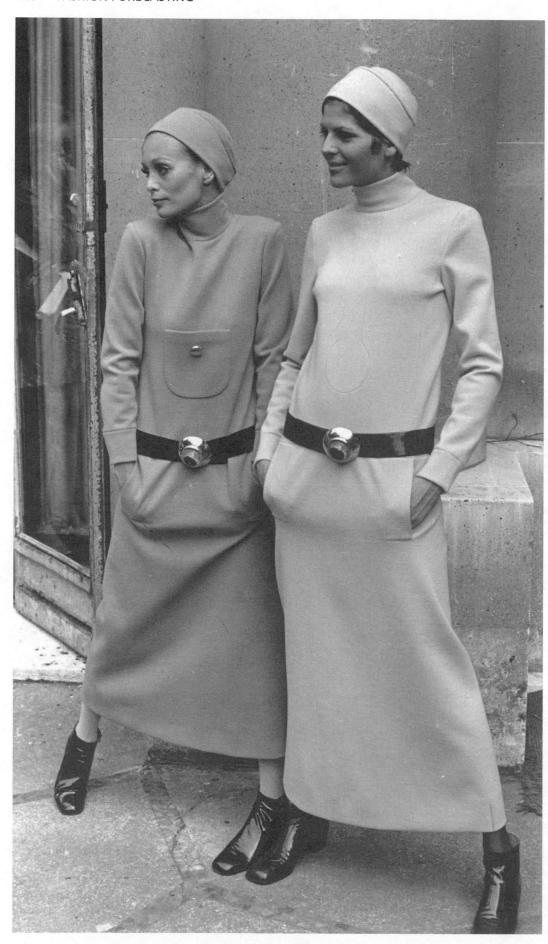

Figure 7.1.
The second era of fashion began in the 1960s with a tilt toward youthfulness and the ready-to-wear revolution. Pierre Cardin was an innovative designer and marketer. His visionary 1968 collection is shown here. (Corbis Images)

● CASE STUDY
From Catwalk to Main Street

Karla began her career in retailing where her flair for fashion led to a position as fashion director for a 16-store chain in the midwestern United States. The stores target young women with trendy, fashion-forward apparel presented in a lifestyle concept that covers categories from prom dresses to casual, weekend clothes. As fashion director, Karla's function is to translate the season's fashion story into one specifically targeted to her store's customers, location, and price points.

Karla begins by gathering information about trends from the runways, showrooms, and streets. She attends seasonal shows at the Apparel Mart in her part of the country, always looking for new resources to set her stores apart from others in the same market. She also attends trade shows in New York and Los Angeles and researches fashion trends in Europe one or two times each year. From these activities and sources, she synthesizes all the emerging trends into an overall fashion story, seasonal theme, and merchandising direction for the stores. She communicates her findings to the buyers and other executives in the corporate offices in a seminar using visuals of runway shows, store windows, and street fashion. The fashion story is also available to the chain's executives on the company's intranet—a proprietary network using Internet technology. She repeats the seminars for sales associates at each store in the chain at the beginning of the new season just as the new merchandise begins to arrive in the stores.

Karla's role expanded when the chain decided to launch a private-label line. The goal was to make the selling floor distinctive with fashion products not available at any other stores. The chain contracted with a product development company that would handle all the design and production of the products. Karla became the fashion link between the two companies. Now on her trips in the United States and Europe, she looks for fashion ideas that can be adapted for the private-label line.

This chapter covers the research and decision-making process Karla uses in developing the fashion story and customizing it for her chain.

fee arrangement with the designers, acquired models for manufacturing at lower prices in their own countries.

The absolute dictatorship of fashion by Paris was undermined in the 1920s. Early in the decade Coco Chanel popularized "the poor look" of simple dresses, jersey suits, sweaters, cloche hats, and pants. Jean Patou introduced the sportswear approach to fashion, which he described as follows: "I have aimed at making [my clothes] pleasant to the eye and allowing absolute liberty of movement." These looks replaced the elaborate fashions and constricting stays that kept women sedentary with a new aesthetic ideal for the modern woman—slim, active, athletic. Chanel's "poor look" and Patou's sportswear were also much easier to imitate, thereby opening up fashionability to more consumers.

Daytime dress became more comfortable and functional, but evening fashion continued to be the epitome of seductive femininity. This fracturing of looks played out in ever more varied forms. A woman could choose to be a sexy woman, a "schoolgirl" in black dress with white collar and cuffs, a professional woman in a tailored suit, or a sporty woman in trousers and a sweater set. After the 1920s, the unity of a single fashion message disappeared; disparate and sometimes opposed looks shared the stage. Fashion gained transformative power as it became possible to manipulate appearance to express self, personality, and individuality—to change the way a woman viewed herself and how other people saw her. Instead of issuing strict injunctions, fashion began to offer a diversified set of options inviting the consumer to choose.

THE SECOND ERA OF MODERN FASHION

The ready-to-wear revolution coincided with a tilt toward youthfulness and novelty as ideals. A two-tiered fashion system emerged with couture focused on masterpieces of execution and ready-to-wear focused on improving manufacturing technology and trend-driven merchandising. Pierre Cardin showed a ready-to-wear line at the French department store Printemps in 1959, opened the first ready-to-wear department in 1963, and was the first to sign licensing agreements with ready-to-wear manufacturers. In 1966, Yves Saint Laurent created the first ready-to-wear line conceived on its own terms and not as an adaptation of haute couture. Emerging new designers like Mary Quant focused primarily on ready-to-wear. During this second era, designers became brand names for a variety of products from apparel to fragrance, accessories to home decor.

The emergence of youth as an ideal brought with it new emphasis on the values of individual expression, spontaneity, and the humor of stylistic collages and juxtapositions. Good taste and the distinctions of class were identified with the "old" order. The cult of youth became intrinsically linked with the cult of the body. Instead of following the latest fashion dictates closely, the consumer became more autonomous. "In" was not defined by aspirations for status or social position but by being "in the know." Clothes could be casual as long as they conveyed a youthful, liberated, and individualized image.

THE THIRD ERA OF MODERN FASHION

The defining characteristics of the third era of modern fashion are diversity in acceptable looks and a blurring of the line between what is "in" and "out" of fashion. Today, all styles are legitimate—pared-down modernism and sexy vamp looks, short and long, tight and loose, "down-and-out" distressed fabrics and refined chic, sneakers and stilettos. During the first two eras of modern fashion, following trends as defined by designers, the press, and merchants was important in presenting an appropriate image to the world. In the third era of modern fashion, a broad range of alternative looks became acceptable and people became less inclined to define "appropriate" in any definite terms.

● ● ● ACTIVITY 7.1. Business Breakthroughs and Classic Designers

Investigate the design and marketing of fashion by influential designers like Paul Poiret, Mariano Fortuny, Jean Patou, Coco Chanel, and Elsa Schiaparelli to discover practices that were revolutionary in their time but are now commonplace ways of doing business. What revolutionary ways of doing business today will become accepted practice in the future?

● ● ● ACTIVITY 7.2. Good Taste/Bad Taste

Go back to original sources published during the Youthquake in the mid-1960s—books of advice on how to dress, magazine and newspaper articles. A debate raged between the adults of the era and young people. Read about what was considered "good" and "bad" taste at the time. Parallel this earlier debate with criticism of fashion looks from today's subcultural groups. Is there a "generation gap" when it comes to fashion today—tweens to teens, teens to young adults, young adults to mature adults? Consider the difference in fashion (popular looks) and style (personal expression). Describe the tastes of the different age segments. Are there looks that bridge the gap by being popular across generational lines?

The seeds of the current era of fashion can be seen in the 1920s when fashion began to fracture into multiple looks and in the 1960s when individualism and consumer autonomy encouraged a proliferation of fashion alternatives. Gone were the days of unitary trends passed from haute couture to the rest of the world. Instead, the fashion world fragmented into multiple trends from multiple centers of creation and popularized by mass media. During the two earlier eras of modern fashion, the distinction between "in" and "out" of fashion was preserved. The loss of this distinction can be seen as a shift between fashion—the following of an accepted norm that fluctuates over time—and style—the pursuit of a personal, individualistic look outside of time-based oscillations (Polhemus, 1996).

The growing autonomy of the consumer and the rejection of fashions touted by designers and the press mean that today, few new styles achieve quick adoption. The pressure for instant assimilation has disappeared. For consumers, the concepts of being "trendy" (i.e., following trends) and being a fashion victim fused (Polhemus, 1996). The wish to avoid both designations

has driven consumers toward individualized selection and mixing of influences. The result of these forces is that while the pace of fashion introduction and the translation of styles into all price points have increased, the speed of adoption has slowed down (Lipovetsky, 1994). Instead of following fashion dictates and trends, consumers filter from the many options and choose those that fit their individual aesthetic. Ironic mixtures of styles and influences define today's fashion. There is no longer a fashion; there are fashions.

Barbara Vinken (2005) builds on Lipovetsky's analysis by identifying 100 years of fashion—from Frederick Worth to Saint Laurent with Schiaperelli and Chanel as the high points—when haute couture expressed modernity and dictated fashion. Beginning in the 1980s, she terms the new era "postfashion" where creative direction comes from *prêt-à-porter* (ready-to-wear), the dictatorial power of the couturier is broken, and fashion becomes a coproduction between the designer and the people who wear the clothes. The aesthetic shifts from fashion as art to fashion as commentary, which fragments and recombines symbols of affluence and poverty, beauty and ugliness.

The idea of fashion as a coproduction between designer and consumer dovetails with the rise of peer-based sources of information. Consumers began to reject the artificial scripts of top-down marketing in favor of "new media" (the Internet and related technologies) and consumer-generated content. The "old media" depended on controlling the message and mass marketing but the new media appealed to a fragmented set of subcultures, each with its own interests (Popcorn, 2005). The new tastemakers became aficionados of a cultural niche who reviewed available products and reported

their opinions on **blogs** (Web logs) and special interest Web sites—a fan-to-fan form of communication that bypassed traditional gatekeepers (Leeds, 2006).

Fashion blogs written by independents (those not associated with magazines or corporations) range from celebrity sightings to street style, shopping guides to runway reviews (see Resource Pointers) (Figure 7.2). The newest category, local style blogs, focuses on identifying the fashion signature of the area and the best sources for that look. Blogs are more current because their reaction time is faster than traditional media (fashion magazines work three or more months in advance of release). Print media reacted by adding blogs to their Web sites (Britten, 2007). Designers reacted by inviting the new media to join the old media at the runway shows in New York, London,

Paris, and Milan—of the approximately 3,500 journalists, 10 percent write for blogs (Thompson Smith, 2007).

Along with the proliferation of user-generated content came questions about its reliability. Iconoculture, a trend advisory service, cited a swing back to expert opinion and professionally edited content for consumers seeking credible sources ("Iconoculture," 2007). One Internet entrepreneur, linking content with the potential for premium audiences and advertising money, said, "The more trusted an environment, the more you can charge for it." The likelihood is that both independent blogs and professional sites will coexist in the evolving Web space (Dokoupil, 2008). The information domain demonstrates the same characteristic as post-fashion, coproduction between creatives and consumers.

Figure 7.2.
Designers invite both representatives of the "new media" and the "old media" to attend runway shows. Bloggers can post fashion news faster than traditional print and broadcast media.
(*WWD*, Courtesy of Fairchild Publications)

Style Tribes

Substituting for the distinction between "in" and "out" in the third era of modern fashion is the distinction of "belonging to" a group, a cluster of like-minded and like-living people. Adopting an appearance style is a marker of membership in a **style tribe** (Polhemus, 1996). Steampunk, a subculture based on a time-traveling fantasy world, is one part retro-romantic and one part technology. Devotees read Jules Verne and H. G. Wells and esteem dirigibles, steam locomotives, vaudeville, and the Victorian Age. Unlike hip-hop and Goth, which seem threatening to outsiders, steampunk may be bizarre, but its quaintness attracts a following. The aesthetic expresses a desire for formality, refinement, and ritual—adherents attend tea parties and time-traveler balls. The style incorporates music, film, design, and fashion. The look fuses current fashion with neo-Edwardian touches like a gentleman's waistcoat and paisley bow tie and extends to a brass-encased iPhone. For women, the look is built on corsets, bustles, crinolines, and parasols. Favored designers include Nicoloas Ghesquiere of Balenciaga, Alexander McQueen, and Ralph Lauren. Emerging in the early-1990s as a taste in literature, steampunk has grown into a worldview supported by its own Internet culture, handmade clothing designers, and retailers (La Ferla, 2008b).Group membership as conveyed by a "uniform" is not a new idea—

hippies of the 1970s dressed to convey their unmaterialistic value system (Wintour, 1998b). Although the appearance style of this group has blurred into a stereotype, there were actually separate style tribes within the hippie look, including the flower child, African-influenced styles, groups with a political agenda, and others.

Style tribes can be found in the subcultural groups that give rise to street fashion. A version of the same phenomenon is at work when the social clusters in a high school can be recognized by the cultural uniform they wear—rebels, skateboarders, or preps (Sullivan, 1998). People in technological or creative fields often evolve a "uniform" look, even down to the preferred brand names for each item. Occupational clusters, groups sharing a special interest from stock car racing to bird-watching, cliques with the same taste in fashion and decor—all of these and many more are style tribes.

Designers act as style tribe leaders when they present a signature style that appeals to consumers who share that aesthetic and not to others. Designers such as Ralph Lauren, Marc Jacobs, Nicole Miller, and others have a signature style recognizable to even a casual observer.

Some specialty stores and brands appeal directly to style tribes through their selection of merchandise and the design of their bricks-and-mortar and online stores. Department

● ● ● ACTIVITY 7.3. Blog Locally

Does your locale have a style signature? Is there a preference pattern shared by consumers and catered to by local stores? Read some of the blogs that focus on regional differences and decide if your area deserves its own style blog. Brainstorm with class members on the content of the site and begin a trial version available only to fellow students. If the site proves viable, roll it out on the Web. Contact the local press and store owners to publicize the site.

stores and the Gap appeal to a broad spectrum of shoppers, but some specialty stores create teen-friendly shopping environments and Web sites focused on specific teen subcultures. The goal is to "allow [teens] to be part of the brand and image" (Weitzman, 2001) (Figure 7.3).

The Role of the Forecaster

The proliferation of trends in this third era of modern fashion creates a more cluttered information environment for today's fashion forecaster. Because consumers' decisions are less restricted by social rules, buying behavior is more difficult to predict. In this third era of modern fashion, a "triple logic" is in effect (Lipovetsky, 1994):

- The logic of aesthetics.
- The logic of industrial clothing manufacturing (Figure 7.4).
- The logic of consumers acting on individual taste.

It is the fashion forecaster's job to sort out the workings of this triple logic. The forecaster appreciates and understands the aesthetics demonstrated in designers' collections and in street fashion. While appreciating the art, the forecaster edits away the theatrical trappings to discover the wearable clothes underneath. Wearable relates both to the industrial logic of being reproduced at lower price points and

Figure 7.3.
Once the exclusive style of upper-class Ivy Leaguers, the preppy look was appropriated as a status symbol and lifestyle statement by college students. Capitalizing on the style's tribe characteristics, Ralph Lauren's Rugby stores, like this one on Newbury Street in Boston, offer head-to-toe preppy looks for men and women. (*WWD*, Courtesy of Fairchild Publications)

Figure 7.4.
Forecasters looking for trends must consider how styles can be produced within the industrial manufacturing complex and at price levels that are acceptable to consumers.
(*WWD*, Courtesy of Fairchild Publications)

● ● ● ● ACTIVITY 7.4. Style Tribes on Campus

Conduct visual research on the style tribes on your campus or in your town. Take candid photographs of groups of people on the street. How many style tribes can you identify? Do not settle for a superficial reading of the cues. Look for differences in the fine details of footwear, logos, fabrications, straps, and toggles.

satisfying the needs of consumers' lifestyles. Clothes that are wearable for one consumer are impossible for another. The forecaster's understanding of aesthetics, manufacturing, and what is considered wearable from the consumer's point of view leads to a forecast.

Fashion forecasting requires three competencies:

- Proficiency in researching fashion developments using the tools of environmental scanning.
- The ability to identify the visual and symbolic core concepts within and across collections.
- The expertise to analyze the match between fashion developments and the marketplace and to synthesize an actionable forecast for a client.

Information is gathered in the research phase from many sources, among them: attending fashion shows and trade events, as well as gleaning fashion news from print, broadcasting, and online channels. These sources are sifted for **core concepts** or trends. Core concepts are culturally expressive ideals that are endlessly reinterpreted across seasons, years, and decades. Trends can be defined as similarities across information sources. Next, trends are analyzed to determine the potential match with consumer profiles. The consumer profile must go beyond demographics (e.g., age, gender, income level, occupational title) to the subtle differences in personal philosophy as expressed in lifestyle, group membership, preferences, and taste (Polhemus, 1996). Finally, the elements are assembled into an actionable forecast by product category, price point, and retail concept. An actionable forecast is plausible and detailed enough to support executive decisions on design (the logic of aesthetics and manufacturing) and assortment planning (the logic matching style and price to consumer lifestyles).

The Fashion Map

As fashion insiders, forecasters have a mental map of the marketplace—the locations where innovations are likely to be glimpsed early, the supply chain of the textile/apparel industry, and the retail conduit to consumers. Fashion insiders also have another mental map—the map of seasons and shows. When consumers shop for winter coats or summer swimsuits, fashion insiders are seasons ahead in their thinking. Forecasters use these mental maps to organize their observation of directional information. Because innovations rarely apply to the entire marketplace, information must be tagged for the appropriate price point, category, and classification. In this way, forecasters turn random bits of data into useful information for decision support.

● ● ● ● ACTIVITY 7.5. Editing the Avant-Garde

Using online sources that report on fashion, capture images from two or three of the most avant-garde collections from couture and ready-to-wear (see the Resource Pointers at the end of this chapter for suggestions). Mentally strip away the theatrical trappings. Are there wearable clothes underneath? What styles from these avant-garde collections could meet the "industrial logic" of being reproduced at lower price points for consumers? What types of consumers are likely to relate to the aesthetics of these fashion looks?

FASHION GEOGRAPHY

Fashion leadership is no longer exclusively a French commodity. Today, the fashion world is global with design centers in many countries. However, some design centers have special cachet. They are made distinctive by their design heritage and by the aesthetic that they represent (Hastreiter, 1997).

French Luxe

French fashion traces its roots to haute couture, one-of-a-kind showpieces made by skilled dressmakers for a particular client. In the first half of the twentieth century, fashion spoke only French. The first years of the century, *la Belle Époque*, represents the high-water mark for class-conscious extravagance with ribbons, laces, flowers, feathers, and jewels. Haute couture, with its focus on artistry and workmanship, has continued as a tradition of French fashion and filters down to luxury labels of Paris ready-to-wear (Figure 7.5). With the Chambre Syndicale, French fashion's governing board, and support from the French government, designers made Paris the fashion capital for luxury.

American Sportswear

When the Nazis occupied Paris during World War II, the United States was cut off from Paris's influence and American fashion came into its own as the center of sportswear design (Brubach, 1998; Tapert, 1998). Sportswear presented an alternative tradition by substituting practicality, casual comfort, and dash for virtuoso cut, custom fabrics, and embellishment. American sportswear has its roots in mass-produced clothes such as jeans and off-the-peg clothes from the department store. Whereas French couture focused on artistry, American sportswear focused on the changing lifestyles of women. Claire McCardell, an American designer of the 1940s, is credited with offering women a more casual, active, and less constricted view of what a modern woman should wear. The look of American fashion was confirmed in the 1970s with the emergence of Halston's simple but sophisticated cuts, Calvin Klein's minimalism, Ralph Lauren's idealized nostalgia, and Donna Karan's career woman wardrobe (Alfano, 2003). Today, American sportswear is a paradigm—luxurious without being ostentatious, styled for women who want clothes that make sense (Figure 7.6). This paradigm has spread around the world as casual, sporty, unconstructed styles.

British Edge

The high point for British influence on fashion came in the 1960s when young people exploded the repressive English class system, bent on self-expression in music and clothing. This was the first wave of street fashion to make its way into mainstream fashion. Mods and Carnaby Street, Mary Quant and Biba (a boutique showcase for young fashion) still echo in today's fashion world. British art schools that nurtured the talents of John Galliano, Alexander McQueen, and Stella McCartney continue to graduate designers who fill London boutiques with ironic, hip, and radical fashion (Trebay, 2002). British fashion tends to take center stage when the accent is on youthful fashion and translation of street fashion (Figure 7.7).

Figure 7.5.
French fashion is known for its focus on artistry and workmanship, a tradition that can be traced to its roots in haute couture (Dior). (*WWD*, Courtesy of Fairchild Publications)

Figure 7.6.
American sportswear, with its roots in mass-produced clothing, offers practicality that fits with an active lifestyle (Michael Kors). (*WWD*, Courtesy of Fairchild Publications)

Figure 7.7.
British fashion came into its own with the street fashion of the 1960s and continues to be thought of as youthful, whimsical, and hip (Temperley London).
(*WWD*, Courtesy of Fairchild Publications)

Italian Ease

From small family-run artisan mills to multimillion-dollar factories, Italian fashion developed from a tradition of fine fabrics from the Como, Biella, and Prato regions, and leather from Tuscany. Italian design was influential in the 1950s when the Fontana sisters created fashions for Hollywood actresses like Elizabeth Taylor and Gina Lollobrigida (Feitelberg, 2003). Italian design resurfaced in the 1970s when designers such as Giorgio Armani, Gianni Versace, and Missoni moved to center stage. The Italian look has always been a blend between quality and design—softer, more textured, and less hard-edged than French fashion (Figure 7.8).

Japanese Cut

The radical modernism of the Japanese designers such as Issay Miyake, Rei Kawakubo, and Yohji Yamamoto emerged in the 1980s offering a sculptural alternative to the heavy French structures and the softer Italian styles. The Japanese designers relied on high-tech fabrics and finishes and unusual cuts and wrapping effects (Figure 7.9). Their innovations sparked the movement toward deconstruction and minimalism that continues to influence fashion.

Belgian Individuality

Ann Demeulemeester, Martin Margiela, Dries Van Noten, and Veronique Branquinho all trace their fashion roots to Antwerp. The first of the Belgian designers came to prominence in the 1980s. Their work is defined by structural cuts and tailoring in a deconstructed mode (Figure 7.10).

Whereas some of the traditional roots of fashion are still visible in the collections shown in Paris, London, Milan, and New York, the design world is much more complex these days (Foley, 1998). The city where a designer is based is less descriptive than it used to be—designers of many nationalities work in all the fashion centers and designers show in multiple capitals in a single season. Each season new designers emerge and established designers change houses. The same designer may create their own lines plus lines for other houses. The forecaster must revise the fashion map every season. Clients, buyers, and journalists arrive at the shows in Paris, London, Milan, and New York with expectations based on the visual signature of each capital. And, no matter where they show, designers are categorized in part by their creative origin.

● ● ● ACTIVITY 7.6. Fashion Capitals

Use Internet coverage on each of the fashion capitals—Paris, Milan, London, and New York—to analyze the visual signature (see Resource Pointers). Does each fashion capital have its own style niche? What designers epitomize each fashion capital? Which designers are outside the tradition of each fashion capital? What are the aesthetic commonalities between designers of the same nationality—American, French, Italian, British, Belgian, German, and Japanese? What cultural factors contribute to these commonalities?

Figure 7.8.
Italian fashion is known for the rich, luxury fabrics of wool and silk and for high-quality workmanship with a softer edge than that of French fashion (Giorgio Armani). (*WWD*, Courtesy of Fairchild Publications)

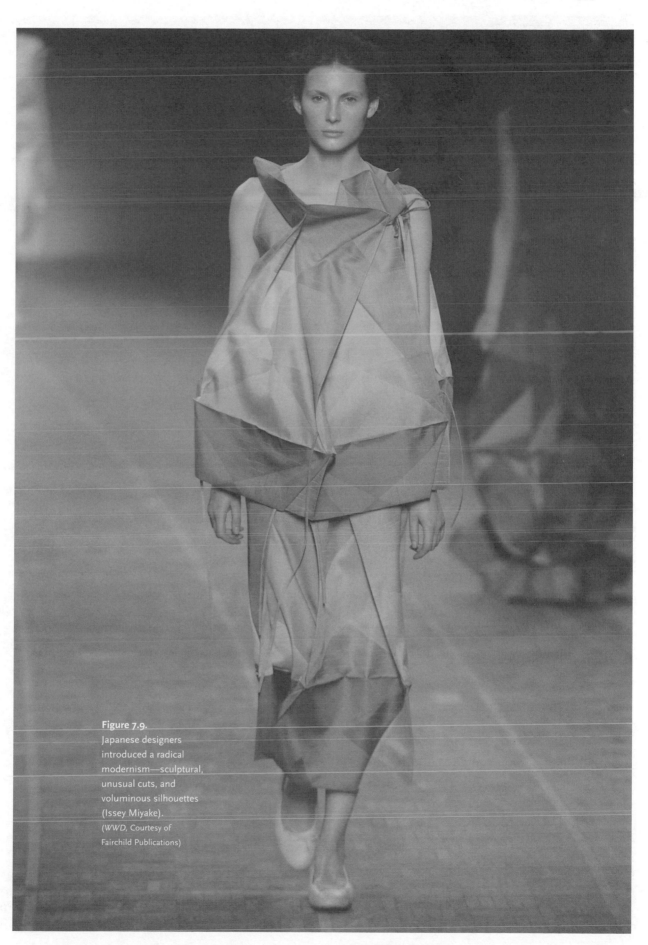

Figure 7.9.
Japanese designers
introduced a radical
modernism—sculptural,
unusual cuts, and
voluminous silhouettes
(Issey Miyake).
(*WWD*, Courtesy of
Fairchild Publications)

Figure 7.10.
Belgian designers
are known for structural
cuts, tailoring, and
a modern deconstructed
look (Veronique
Branquinho).
(*WWD*, Courtesy of
Fairchild Publications)

Figure 7.11.
Covering fashion weeks means seeing hundreds of shows in the four fashion capitals and identifying trends emerging from the multitude of images. (*WWD*, Courtesy of Fairchild Publications)

Fashion Weeks for Ready-to-Wear

Fashion weeks consist of **runway shows** in each of the four fashion capitals—New York, London, Milan, and Paris. Although not as costly as couture ($1,500 to $5,000 for a jacket), **designer ready-to-wear** is still expensive, luxurious, and beautifully executed. Whereas a couture outfit may be made only once or, at most, a few times, designer ready-to-wear is reproduced in the hundreds or thousands. The designers walk a fine line between playing it safe and getting little press coverage and going over the top with offbeat looks that fail in the stores. Designers in this category get lots of press coverage and their successes and failures are recorded on the scorecard kept by the press.

Some collections leap forward into the fashion future. Other collections work and rework a concept season after season or refine favorite themes over and over. Trends reported in the press often begin here when editors notice underlying similarities across designers' collections, when a designer presents an outstanding collection with a unifying theme, or when an item stars in many shows and becomes newsworthy. A magazine editor, fashion director, or forecaster setting out to cover the collections in a single season would choose between hundreds of shows presented by established and emerging designers and by design houses and brands. Covering the shows means assessing each in terms of the line's history and the spirit of the times, identifying emerging or continuing trends across shows, and spotting the standout outfits that can be used to illustrate the trends (Figure 7.11).

The show schedule is always controversial. The ready-to-wear shows for fall/winter occur in February/March and spring/summer in September/October. The actual dates, placement of shows within the schedule, and logistics depend on negotiation between the show organizers (Chambre Syndicale de la Haute Couture for Paris and Chamber of Fashion for Italy).

Costs for a runway show can run as much as $750,000 (or even $2 million for the most extravagant shows). Although important clients and celebrities are invited to the shows, the real aim is to attract fashion editors' interest and sell to store buyers. If the right people don't see the presentation, the investment in a show is wasted (Murphy, 2001a; Murphy, 2002a).

In each fashion capital a coordinating group arranges the schedule so that key shows don't overlap—British Fashion Council, Council of Fashion Designers of America, Camera Della Moda (Milan), and Fédération Français de la Couture (Paris). In New York designers check with Ruth Finley, publisher of the Fashion Calendar, for possible conflicts before scheduling. Her calendar, with a current subscription price of $425 per year, has been keeping track of shows since 1941 (Wilson, 2007c).

Further complicating the schedule is the overlap between showing the line and beginning development of the future season. Fashion week can clash with fabric shows like Première Vision (PV) in Europe. Some designers leave immediately after their shows and fly to Paris to view the latest in fabric development. Others send members of their design team to Première Vision, attend other fabric shows where dates do not conflict with fashion weeks, or buy fabrics from company representatives or showrooms ("PV," 2002).

The schedule for shows in the fashion capitals will continue to be a controversial issue because the dates must accommodate the requirements of designers, who need time to develop their lines; the merchants, who must place orders; and the press, who must photograph and present the fashion news to the public. The fallout from decisions about timing reverberates down the supply chain to manufacturers of fibers, fabrics, trims, and findings.

In addition to the designers who stage runway shows, other designers participate in trade shows or showroom events. Satellite trade shows for accessories are set to precede, coincide, or follow each fashion week. Paris features a particularly crowded schedule of showings and trade shows. Each trade show in each city fills a niche and targets specific retailers. For example, the Paris trade show Atmosphére features designers who are fashion forward and directional and targets retailers with smaller fashion boutiques. For designers, showing in this trade show is often a stepping-stone to international import markets. Merchants and journalists must find time in a hectic schedule of runway shows to also cover the trade shows.

Although fashion shows may look glamorous, they are also often crowded, hot, smoky, presented at hard-to-get-to venues, and frequently start late. They can be a circus to get into (Trebay, 2002). This exhausting round of 18-hour days takes its toll on the attendees. Most report going into training in preparation for this biannual burst of focused action.

An alternative is to see the shows online. Companies specialize in covering runway shows on subscription and no-fee sites. StyleSight provides 2 million images from the latest designer runway shows to subscribers who pay $15,000 per year for access (Jana, 2007). Still, it is unlikely that television or online will replace seeing the shows in person because the runway pictures cannot convey the total experience (Braunstein, 2001).

Travel doesn't have to end with the last Paris show. Journalists and buyers can continue on to cover fashion weeks in Australia (especially strong for swimsuit styling), São Paulo (Brazil), Berlin (Germany), and Copenhagen (Denmark). These second-tier cities are especially valuable to retailers looking for unique lines for their stores and to journalists and forecasters taking a more global look at fashion concepts (Huntington, 2001). Each city adds its own flavor to the fashion picture. The Nordic Fashion Association (Sweden, Norway, Iceland, Finland, and Denmark) aims to become the leader in the combining of fashion, healthy living, and sustainable energy (Groves, 2008b). Fashion week in Berlin highlights the city as an emerging creative hub (Drier & McGuinness, 2007). New fashion weeks are being added constantly. Ann Watson, fashion director of Henri Bendel, attends many and explains: "Fashion has become so global that more and more countries are using fashion weeks as a way to unleash the creativity in their cultures." Many of these emerging fashion capitals pay fashion journalists to travel to their shows (Wilson, 2008d).

Los Angeles Fashion Week

Los Angeles is considered a secondary fashion city when compared to New York, London, Milan, and Paris, but its fashion district rivals New York's in size, it has a reputation for originating trends, and it has a skilled workforce who are mostly Asian in origin (Menkes, 2003a; Oblena, 2003). Los Angeles Fashion Week is mounted as a centralized event organized by *7th on Sixth* (the same group that organizes New York shows) and features both women's and men's lines. Suzy Menkes (2003), reporting for the *International Herald Tribune,* defined the "L.A. look" as more upbeat and colorful than

New York with three facets: a "quirky indie spirit," a "gritty, cool side," and a "vintage style that had been building since the 1970s." Another feature of California fashion is celebrity lines—stars from movies, music, and television moonlighting as designers (Chammas, 2008).

Men's Ready-to-Wear

Designers with both women's wear and menswear lines often show a mix of the two on the catwalk. However, there are designated biannual fashion weeks for menswear in London, New York, Milan, and Paris—January for fall/winter and June for spring/summer (Ageorges, 2003). Because of its history with traditional menswear fabrics and design, Milan is usually considered the most important of these events. To the uninitiated, menswear doesn't seem to change much from season to season but the changes are just more subtle. Trends for menswear fashion are defined by the style (traditional or modern), the attitude (cool, hip, or edgy), the fit, including the length of the jacket, the width of the lapels, the placement of the collar notch and buttons, the number of buttons, pocket and vent details, and fabric color and pattern. Traditional looks feature full tailoring while modern styles are lighter, softer, and less constructed (Gellers, 1999).

Couture

Made-to-measure for the most discriminating clients in the world, **haute couture** features the finest fabrics, embroideries, and workmanship in fashion. Style changes introduced in couture include the replacement of full crinoline by the bustle (Worth), the lean look displacing the corseted hourglass (Poiret), the little black dress (Chanel), the bias cut (Vionnet), the New Look (Dior), the chemise (Balenciaga), the space-inspired minidress (Courrèges and Cardin), and many more (Milbank, 1985). In 1929, there were 91 couture houses with a clientele of 20,000. When designer ready-to-wear exploded in 1967, the number of couture houses plummeted from 37 to 19. Today less than a dozen houses cater to about 500 people who can pay $80,000 for a dress (Horyn, 2007). According to Suzy Menkes, veteran fashion journalist for the *International Herald Tribune*, the future of haute couture is not threatened by the cheapness of "fast fashion"—superwealthy women will always want the best in creativity and craftsmanship—but couture is threatened by time because few women will fly to Paris, participate in multiple fittings, and wait six weeks for delivery (Menkes, 2008a).

Clients pay $20,000 for a couture suit from a major house. In return, a client gets a suit made by hand from scratch exclusively for her. The fabrics will be exquisite, the garment will be fitted to her figure (requiring up to seven fittings), tailored and lined for a flawless silhouette (silk suits are sometimes lined with cashmere), and decorated and embroidered by master artisans. A jacket may take 130 hours of skilled labor to produce, and a ball gown 300 hours or more. The result is a light, virtually weightless garment—an effect that can't be reproduced in machine-made clothing (Rubenstein, 1998). Karl Lagerfeld explains that the couture package includes more than the clothes: "Couture is about service, the salon, the vendeuse, the box, the way the clothes are wrapped and presented to the client" (Horyn, 2003).

Haute couture shows are held in Paris after designer ready-to-wear for the same selling season—January for spring and July for fall / winter collections. Because haute couture is made-to-order for specific clients, it does not require the lead-time for manufacturing that ready-to-wear clothes do. Houses showing couture collections are not all based in Paris. If designers can meet the criteria set by the Chambre Syndicale, then they are allowed to participate.

Shows not on the official couture calendar, "off-calendar" shows, feature new couturiers hoping to attract clients and make the leap onto the couture calendar in the future. Luxury jewelry firms often unveil collections during couture weeks because the clientele overlaps (Socha, 2003).

The death knell for couture has been sounded many times given the prices, shrinking number of couture houses, and small client base. But beginning in the mid-1990s with John Galliano at Dior, interest in couture revived. Journalists point to the commercial demands of ready-to-wear as a limiting factor on creativity while couture is a creative undertaking. Although it may be a cliché to say that couture is a fashion "laboratory" for design, it is true that looks from couture collections do spin off into ready-to-wear (Horyn, 2002). Hollywood stylists looking for the perfect runway dress for their clients help swell the client base for couture (Horyn, 2007).

The couture loses money, but owners feel that costs are justified given the promotional boost the attention brings to fragrance, licensed lines, and ready-to-wear. Because it can be experimental, couture is directional for fashion themes, references to designers and eras of the fashion past, ethnic influences, silhouettes, fabrics, and colors.

● ● ● ACTIVITY 7.7. Couture in Review

Using trade publications, fashion magazines, and the Internet, examine the couture season one, three, and five years ago. Compare these seasons with today's trends in designer ready-to-wear and bridge (the price point just below designer). How is the inspiration and experimentation in couture translated into later collections?

FASHION OFF THE RUNWAY

Established designers will always be on the runway, but the chaos of fashion week and the overcrowded schedule (100 or more shows in each of the fashion capitals) sometimes swamp smaller designer labels and those of emerging talents. Designers who choose not to present their collections on the catwalks save the huge costs in time, money, effort, and distraction, but they also miss out on the visibility, magazine attention, and coverage on television and the Internet. Instead, these designers invite stores and magazines to come to the showroom or send them look-books (photographs of the line). Showroom visits provide a chance for designers to present their point of view more completely than they can in a runway show (Wilson, 2002).

The costs of a runway show during fashion week also do not make sense for well-established brands like Jones Apparel Group, Liz Claiborne, Guess, and St. John (Lockwood, 2003). Citing the shift in emphasis at the shows from retailers to the press, mainstream brands would rather focus on presenting the line to retailers in the showroom and using advertising to stimulate consumer interest.

Showrooms

When a forecaster, magazine editor, or retail buyer talks about scouting the market, he or she often refers to visiting the **showrooms** of designers, manufacturers, and entrepreneurs in the Fashion Center (also known as the Garment District) of New York City. The Fashion Center has the highest concentration and greatest diversification of apparel resources. Open on weekdays throughout the year, the Fashion Center allows a fashion professional to discover new trends and new resources. Not only a district for seeing apparel lines, the businesses run the gamut from agents for European fabric houses to suppliers for trimmings, belts, buttons, and other findings.

Boutiques

Emerging designers newly graduated from school or from apprenticeships as assistants to well-known designers need a retail showcase. They find it by opening small boutiques in fashion's capital cities. These shops are usually found in arty, edgy, fashion-forward enclaves clustered with the boutiques of other designers, vintage apparel stores, bars, and restaurants. SoHo in New York was one such neighborhood starting in the 1970s, but it evolved into today's showcase for European and American brands. When that happens, the avant-garde multibrand specialty stores and new designers migrate to emerging areas like the meatpacking district (west of Ninth Street in the West Village), NoLIta (north of Little Italy), and Alphabet City (avenues A, B, C, and D in the East Village) (Caplan, 2001; Ozzard, 2001).

One of the original fashion neighborhoods, London's Carnaby Street, once the focus of mod fashion in the 1960s, degenerated to selling cheap tourist souvenirs until it became a retail magnet for denim brands, but it wouldn't attract fashion-forward customers without independent boutiques and chic cafés. The retail mix includes unbranded stores (stores owned and stocked by brands but selling specialty products like vintage or limited-edition lines) and concept stores (stores selling cult sneakers, street-inspired looks, or secondary lines by name designers). The real estate management company that owns the properties actively recruits small, innovative retailers by offering competitive rents, store fixtures, and short leases (Jones, 2007a).

New designers also find a showcase in multibrand specialty stores with a reputation for discovering design talent. In the specialty stores, the fashion is often mixed with an in-store café, gallery space for art, objects, fashion, and accessories in a unique retail concept (Raper & Weisman, 1998). One such stop in Paris is Colette on the chic Rue St. Honoré (Figure 7.12). The store also features art exhibits, magazines and books, and a café (Jackson, 1998). Sarah Lerfel, who runs the store, puts it this way: "We want to surprise our customers and show them things that they shouldn't necessarily find elsewhere. We want to open our doors more to the independents and support creativity" (Murphy, 2002b). Fashion-forward boutiques can be found in major cities worldwide—Dover Street Market in London, Corso Cuomo in Milan, Verso in Antwerp, Podium Concept in Moscow—and upscale resort destinations (Fraser-Cavassoni, 2008). Frequented not only by customers but also by the fashion press and forecasters, the visual presentation, product mix, and styles are directional for trendspotters.

Trade Shows

Almost every week of the year somewhere in the world there is an apparel trade show. There are trade shows for:

- All categories of apparel—women's, men's, and children's.
- Categories of accessories.
- Niche and specialty categories such as ecologically conscious vendors.
- Private-label manufacturers.
- Special sizes—plus sizes and petites.

Figure 7.12.
Multibrand specialty stores like Colette in Paris have a reputation for discovering design talent and showcasing trends.
(*WWD*, Courtesy of Fairchild Publications)

Trade shows are centered on selling fashion but they also showcase new design talent and identify trends for specific product categories, price points, and target audiences. Seminars at the shows provide a venue for networking among apparel executives and for discussion of issues that have an impact on the apparel industry.

New York trade shows coincide with the line releases by manufacturers—January (summer), late February to early March (early fall merchandise known as Fall I), late March to early April (fall merchandise known as Fall II), August (holiday and/or resort), and November (spring merchandise). These shows (e.g. Fashion Coterie, and Designers & Agents) allow buyers from around the country to see a wide range of lines. The trade shows feature name designers' lines, lines by young designers, and international contingents from Brazil, Australia, South Korea, and Turkey (Greenberg, 2003).

The shows are especially important for independent stores because they offer a chance to see many lines and select merchandise that differentiates the independents from the large department store chains. As one buyer puts it: "The items [we look for] really have to be one of a kind with maybe a technical aspect of great fabric, and also something that's not carried by everyone" (Larson, 2003). Buyers use the New York trade shows to place orders for immediate delivery and to order for the upcoming season. For many buyers, the shows offer a chance to crystallize trends into specific lines and items customized for their location and customer. For buyers and forecasters, the trade shows offer a way to get an overview of seasonal trends in a more convenient and concentrated way than the alternative, canvassing individual showrooms.

Regional Markets

Serving the same purpose for buyers who do not come to New York are the **regional markets** around the United States, located in Atlanta, Dallas, Chicago, San Francisco, Los Angeles, Denver, Miami, and other regional centers. Regional market centers lease space to manufacturers and sales representatives who carry multiple lines in permanent showrooms and for seasonal shows.

Planned to make buying easier and more convenient for smaller department stores and specialty stores, these marts have evolved as sites where merchandise aligns closely with the needs and preferences of different regions. Manufacturers use regional markets to test the direction of lines and to test the market response to items. Entrepreneurs in the middle price points often begin by showing at regional marts to test the viability of their design direction. Forecasters and buyers for large department store chains use regional markets to explore local market trends that may not show up in national buying patterns.

In addition to the well-known designers and apparel manufacturers showing at regional markets, such shows provide a showcase for designers working far from the runways on the fringes of the market. One such trendsetting concentration for contemporary clothing is in southern California. Working outside the fashion establishment, these designers specialize in the "California look"—body conscious and active looks that display a gym-toned body, ethnic-inspired looks, and ironic combinations (things not usually thought to be compatible). The result is inexpensive contemporary clothing, sophisticated junior wear, and more directional clothes than traditional bridge and career clothes lines. Aimed at independent stores making "smallish buys," these lines epitomize trends toward seasonless fabrics and a casual lifestyle (Steinhauer, 1998a).

STREET FASHION

Street fashion is synonymous with youthful experimentation, with subcultures from cliques to gangs, with the impulse to provoke attention, comment, or reaction (Koda, 2002). Consumers become fashion stylists when they take available clothing resources and mix, restyle, and customize items in individualistic and expressive ways. "Street fashion can afford to make mistakes, to change its mind overnight, because it's cheap or on sale or found on the curbside like an orphan," explained artist Ruben Toledo (2002). But the trip from street to mainstream may take decades as it did with hip-hop style—beginning with the music, the look that appropriated items from Tommy Hilfiger and Ralph Lauren collections, to lines such as Phat Farm targeted at hip-hop audiences (Greenberg, 2003). On a similar trajectory, vintage began its evolution from secondhand discards to street

fashion to celebrity icons in the 1970s when consumer stylists mixed finds from flea markets, resale shops, and the family attic. Today, vintage is an industry with trade shows, auctions for couture designs, famous shops in the fashion capitals (like Decades and Lily et Cie in Los Angeles and Resurrection in New York), small shops in nearly every city, and online shops and auctions. Consumer stylists continue to put together unique looks with vintage pieces but today they have to compete with designers shopping for inspiration and celebrity stylists shopping for clients (Hirschberg, 2000).

Although innovative street looks sometimes influence designer collections, for some apparel categories—juniors, contemporary, and denim—virtually all trends derive from street looks. Street looks are influential for casual streetwear and directional for other age groups and categories (Figure 7.13).

Figure 7.13.

Miu Miu uses old-school street art in this urban-influenced collection. (*WWD*, Courtesy of Fairchild Publications)

To research these trends, companies send designers to locales expected to furnish inspiration.

The reputation of Tokyo teens for creating and exploring trends led to "cool hunt" tours—a fashion consultant charges $800 a day to guide design teams to top boutiques where tastemakers shop. The design tourists spend $20,000 or more on clothes and accessories to inspire the next season. Some save time by shipping the finds to factories in China where they are resized for the American and European customer, manufactured, and shipped to stores (Rowley & Tashiro, 2007).

Any city where the focal point for youth is on playful experimentation with fashion can provide trend information. Likely locales feature small, local, nontraditional companies; vibrant street life centered on underground music culture, cafés, and clubs; and shops experimenting with new retail concepts. The retail concepts mix apparel, decorative accessories for the home, and vintage finds in displays reflective of the tastes of the proprietor.

Additional sources for information on street fashion come from forecasting firms, street fashion blogs, Web sites, and trade shows. Forecasting firms scout for images and supply companies with pictures and video. Trade shows bring together small firms with direct ties to street influences.

Some influences from the street are translated directly into manufacturer's lines if the target consumer is likely to identify with the source and is ready to adopt the innovation. But some influences from the street are too raw or too advanced to move directly into the mainstream. These influences instead trickle up from the street to mainstream, eventually appearing in a modified version. Over time, street influence may have a more general effect in inspiring a shift in mood or emphasis.

Trend Identification, Analysis, and Synthesis

Forecasters work for clients as consultants and within corporations. The yearly agenda for a trend forecaster might look like this (Schweiss-Hankins, 1998):

- Trips to Europe to shop key cities, attend international trade shows, and purchase samples—two to four trips per year.
- Trips to trade shows in cities around the United States—six to eight per year.
- Trips to attend fabric previews and markets—two to four per year.
- Purchase trend predictions and color services—four to ten per year.
- Subscribe to fashion magazines and trade journals to stay up-to-date on trends and industry news.
- Attend presentations by fabric mills and other key suppliers.
- Attend meetings of professional organizations such as color forecasting groups.

● ● ● ACTIVITY 7.8. The Market for Fashion

Regional markets and trade shows usually encourage and accommodate the attendance of fashion students. Attend a market or trade show and focus on small manufacturers, emerging design firms, and avant-garde fashion. Report on the potential for these companies and designers to reach larger markets and appeal to broader audiences.

The purpose of all this activity is to organize observations, present findings, and suggest ways to implement these ideas into merchandise targeted toward the customer.

The forecaster sifts through the information using a process called **abstracting** (Fiore & Kimle, 1997). The process consists of identifying underlying similarities (or differences) across ensembles and design collections. The differences and similarities are frequently expressed as:

- The totality of the look—minimalist versus extravagant, feminine versus masculine, sexy versus refined.
- The theme or mood—survivalist versus gothic romanticism.
- A swing in fashion's pendulum—from flared to narrower legs, from functional to frilly.
- The proportions of the apparel pieces— hem length or in-seam length for pants, placement of the waistline, width or fullness of the garments.
- The silhouette—tubular shift, hourglass, blouson, or wedge.
- Point of emphasis—shoulders, bust, waist, derriere, or legs.
- The fit—body hugging, body skimming, body conscious, or loose.
- A specific detail—collar, pocket, lapel, waistband treatment, sleeve, or cuff.
- Exaggeration in the details—the size, shape, color, texture, or pattern at the neckline or hem or on the collar, pockets, or belt.
- A specific trim—beading, embroidery, appliqué, lace, or cording.

- A specific finding—buttons, zipper, or snaps.
- A fabric type—woven or knit, napped, or metallic.
- Fabric finishing—gradation in color dyeing, slashing, or abrading.
- A specific fabric—transparent fabrics, velvet, or jersey.
- A color story—the rise of a dominant color scheme, a shift in mood, or a narrative that ties together the color trends.

The trend may be reported within a product category—dresses or suits—or across categories.

The ability to recognize similarities between garments and between collections is useful in many fashion careers (Fiore & Kimle, 1997):

- Designers, product developers, and buyers abstract across the garments in a group and the groups in a collection so that a visual theme or aesthetic connects the items.
- Sales representatives and marketing executives abstract across the product line to recognize points to be emphasized in selling the line.
- Fashion journalists abstract across multiple collections to identify patterns in the seasonal offerings and visual and symbolic core concepts that can be translated into editorial features.
- Forecasters abstract across multiple collections and across time to identify patterns that indicate fashion change and direction.

VISUAL CORE CONCEPTS

Forecasters are readers of signs and interpreters of meaning. To recognize core concepts when they appear on the runway and in the street, a forecaster must be familiar with the visual sources and the symbolic meanings of fashion. That means understanding the meaning for the originators of the look and for those who appropriate the look for their own use. It is this deep understanding of signs and symbols and how they are used to create meaning that makes the forecast more accurate, meaningful, and actionable.

Designers are inspired by a myriad of influences from new fabrics to travel experiences, art movements to popular culture, street fashion to the spirit and style of a **muse**—a woman who embodies the ideal look for that designer. Identifying the **visual core concept** in an apparel ensemble, a group, a collection, or a season is more than just analyzing the tangible form. It involves active processing of the intangible attributes—references to past fashions or to ethnic costume, the sensuous or sexual connotations, and imaginative and expressive aspects. It is the juxtaposition of familiar symbols with the exotic ones that creates a *frission*—a thrill or quiver that signals something new and different (Craik, 1994).

Some visual core concepts reoccur over and over in fashion. Each reappearance contains something new, along with traces of all that has come before. These perennial visual core concepts can be categorized as follows:

CONCEPTS REFERENCING THE PAST.

Vera Wang's favorite kind of research is buying vintage dresses and swatch books of rare fabrics and embroideries. She explains, "I find an idea, then I study it, evolve it . . . you always have to take it to another level" (Talley, 1998). She is one of many designers who are influenced by fashion from the distant and not-so-distant past.

CONCEPTS REFERENCING ETHNIC SOURCES.

Middle Eastern, Asian, Latin, and African cultures have inspired fashion. However, some of the results have been controversial, with some critics seeing African regalia on white models as politically incorrect and on black models as patronizing. Critics locate the fault in a "detached view" that tries to "simulate" a look instead of integrating or synthesizing it into something "authentic" to its time and place (Spindler, 1997). Still, references to ethnic sources continue in collections as homage to the creativity of naïve artists and as shorthand for the symbolic values of naturalness and authenticity.

● ● ● ACTIVITY 7.9. The Online Street

Find blogs and Web sites that report on street fashion (see Resource Pointers). Some focus on the most fashion-forward consumers who create, explore, and discard trends quickly. Others look at fashion—what people at a particular location wear to express self, their lifestyle, and the times. Compare the two types of street fashion reporting to identify:

- Global trends, those visible at several sites simultaneously.
- Emerging trends, those that trickle from avant-garde to mainstream or from one geographical location to another.

What time lags are involved? Are there some street trends too fashion forward for immediate translation? Why?

CONCEPTS RELATED TO SEXUALITY.

Fashion watchers have long identified the outsider sensibilities of prostitutes as a source of fashion innovation (Field, 1970; Simmel, 1904). Stiletto heels, the use of rouge and lipstick, red nail polish, and women smoking cigarettes all began in the subculture of prostitutes and spread to other classes. Expressions of sexuality go with the attitudes of living outside accepted norms and dressing the part with clothes, hairstyles, makeup, and accessories. The specifics are linked to the time—Carole Lombard in a white bias-cut dress in the 1930s, or Kate Moss in a transparent slip dress in the 1990s. Today's fashion picture includes all the symbols for seduction, including partial nudity, red lips and nails, stiletto heels, and the colors red and black. One of the great contrasts for a collection or a season is gradation between lady-like looks and the vamp (a seductress) or tramp (the fallen woman) (Trebay, 2002). Another contrast that recurs nearly every season is between the gender symbols for masculine and feminine. A man's watch on a slender female wrist, a military uniform stylized for women, a tuxedo, oxford shirt with a tie—when a woman borrows from a man's wardrobe, the effect is a sexy, slightly perverse look.

CONCEPTS REFERENCING SPORTS.

American sportswear grew out of fashions designed for an active lifestyle that included playing sports and being a spectator at sporting events (Figure 7.14). Today, all categories of sports from skateboarding to motocross to extreme sports are referenced in collections for casual and streetwear. Famous brands have usurped many of the looks originated by small manufacturers of adventure gear as apparel for participants in active sports. Some consumers favor the authentic sports apparel that they use as multifunctional pieces for recreation and work. Other consumers are satisfied with the outdoor look in name brand lines ("City slickers," 1998).

CONCEPTS REFERENCING APPROPRIATENESS.

Sometimes referred to as "uptown chic" versus "downtown hip," the concept means that some styles connect with certain places and attitudes. An uptown girl wears a jacket, silk T-shirt, and carries a Hermès bag. A downtown girl wears black jeans, white cotton T-shirt, and high-tech sneakers. Designers tend to relate to one sensibility or another. Labels like "preppy" or "bohemian" reference the establishment, classy and conservative versus the unconventional and rebellious.

AVANT-GARDE CONCEPTS.

Labeled "artsy" by some, original, creative, individual, and surprising innovations are not usually praised or accepted. Avant-garde designers frequently have a point of view that comments on the issues of the day (Betts, 1998b). Few really avant-garde styles are sold or worn. However, these ideas sometimes have a long-lasting impact on fashion. Examples include Rudi Gernreich, Paco Rabanne, Andre Courrèges, and Pierre Cardin in the mid-1960s, as well as Japanese and Belgian designers in the 1990s. Designers who work in the space between art and commerce appeal to the individualists and intellectuals among fashion insiders. Their appeal to a larger public is negligible. Their work often references architecture. Other style points include intricate draping, wrapping, and pleating, asymmetry, unconventional fastenings, unusual fabrics, and sculptural effects.

Figure 7.14.
Playing sports, being a spectator, or just wanting a sporty look keep consumers buying styles associated with sports from tennis to motocross. (*WWD*, Courtesy of Fairchild Publications)

THE CONCEPT OF MODERNITY. The term **modernity** refers to the aesthetic that emerged with technological innovations such as the automobile, telephone, plastics, synthetic dyes, and man-made fibers, and with mass media and entertainment such as the movies. Collections with modernity as a theme strenuously avoid any reference to past fashion. Instead, they focus on sleekness, banishment of frills, functional details, and performance and technical fabrics.

THE CONCEPT OF POSTMODERN.
Postmodern culture is associated with an emerging global economy, fragmentation in society, extreme eclecticism in the use of signs and symbols, unease with the consequences

of modernity, and fluidity in social identities. Collections with a postmodern inclination focus on mixing symbols from different cultures and times or on the protective function of clothing. As designer Jil Sander puts it: "We don't know what the future will bring. We're confused and almost feel lost in our mass consumer society with its global information system" (Cooper, 1998). The design response is to create clothing that is a mad mix of all that has gone before or that functions as a utilitarian personal habitat.

Abstracting means recognizing the symbolic and visual core concepts in a garment, a collection, or a season. But the forecaster must go beyond merely recognizing the core concepts to putting them in the perspective of fashion

visual core concepts represent trends and how those trends are likely to play out in the future.

Whether the forecaster is working inside a company or as a consultant, the reporting from all the travel, observation, and interpretation is a trend presentation. If the company creates branded or private-label lines, the audience will include product developers. If the company is a retailer, the audience will include buyers who select from the lines of national brands of those products that match the trends. Marketing, promotion, and sales staff will attend so that they can present the merchandise within the contest of trends. The attendees should leave the presentation understanding how the current trends fit with the company's identity and the customer's lifestyle.

DIFFERENT DESIGNERS WITH THE SAME DESIGN CONCEPT

Designers are presumed to be creators and originators. Their goal is to build a recognized branded image that consumers identify with and feel loyal to. They work independently and cloak their collections in secrecy until they are revealed on the catwalk. How then do designers in a given season so often end up with similar design concepts, themes, and moods for the season?

Zeitgeist

The usual answer to this question is Zeitgeist— the trend is in the air, and it is part of the spirit of the times (see Chapter 1). Listen to designers talking in the same buzzwords about a given season's style, fabrics, and fit. Tomas Maier, designer for Bottega Venata, said that he "got a click on the armor" while visiting a museum. Then how does one explain the articulated sleeves in the Jil Sander show and the chain mail looks in Karl Lagerfeld's designs for Fendi in the same season? Each season some inspiration clicks for designers "independently but somehow in unison" (Trebay, 2003).

Synchronicity can also partly be explained because designers attend the same fabric trade shows and those trade shows feature the directions anticipated by leading forecasting agencies (Freeman, 2002).

Designers do inhabit the same cultural strata—read the same periodicals, attend the same parties, know many of the same people, and know which movies and plays are "hot" topics of conversation among the media elite. Because designers are experiencing the same cultural current, it is only natural that these influences will foreshadow fashion change and lead to some similarities in the collections.

Designer's Designer

A few designers in each era are highly original talents who experiment with new design directions. Paul Poiret, Coco Chanel, Madeleine Vionnet, Charles James, Christian Dior, Yves Saint Laurent, and Andre Courrèges were such designers in their eras. Christian Lacroix's 1987 debut with his pouf skirts and madcap mixes of color and pattern introduced something new and directional. The emergence of Japanese designers in the late 1980s played an influential role in setting the design agenda for the early 1990s. Beginning in the late 1990s, Ann Demeulemeester, Martin Margiela, and Helmut Lang played this role. These are the designer's designers—the ones who influence other designers.

Today's version of the breed creates

● ● ● ACTIVITY 7.10.

Deconstructing a Designer's Core Concepts

Select a designer and deconstruct the visual and symbolic core concepts in the most recent collections. Prepare a presentation board showing the original source referenced in the collection and the translation of that source by the designer. Compare to other designers referencing similar sources.

David Wolfe, Doneger Creative Services

David Wolfe began his career in 1959 in Ohio but he soon became one of Europe's leading fashion illustrators, "European ready-to-wear styles were becoming interesting to American designers and retailers, and there was a hunger for this king of information. [Forecasters] were like foreign correspondents, only for fashion" (Zimmerman, 2008). He switched to the fashion forecasting industry in the late 1960s: Wolfe later became the Creative Director of D3 (Doneger Design Direction), a color and fashion trend-forecasting service.

Unlike many forecasting services, Doneger began as a traditional buying office but morphed into a fashion merchandising and trend-forecasting organization positioning itself as the "one-stop shop" for retailers, manufacturers, and designers. Doneger Group has acquired 18 companies since 1980 including Here & Now, a fashion information service that collects fabric swatches and styles from around the world for use by product developers; Tobe, publisher of *The Tobe Report*, which provides an industry overview of trends; and Directives West, the West Coast point of view in junior, contemporary, and young men's fashion (Casabona, 2007; Moin, 2006; Moin, 2008).

The Doneger Group provides trend and forecasting services through Creative Services, headed by Wolfe. The staff of 20 forecasters brings global market trend analysis to the fashion industry in presentations, consulting, and publications. The division has over 400 subscribers. When adding to the staff, Wolfe says, it is "a red flag to me when I'm hiring someone who says 'my whole life is fashion.' You have to be interested in much more than fashion. You have to understand the world if you are going to understand what people want to wear" (Zimmerman, 2008).

Wolfe's perspective on fashion comes from observing change over time. He thinks fashion is changing more slowly now than it did when he began his career. According to Wolfe, the fashion business "was so easy then; it is so difficult now" because then "there were rules, it was organized, we had a consumer population who was obsessed and obedient—they're not even listening to us anymore!" (1998). He sees style today in a holding pattern where most consumers, male and female, are content with the familiar.

Wolfe (1999) characterizes most of the twentieth century as about upward style mobility—"No matter where you were on the economic or social strata, you looked up, up, up." But a few decades ago fashion began to look downward to the street for inspiration. He even goes further back in tracing the shift: "I think Levi Straus invented the garment that was the watershed turning point in fashion. He's responsible for the entire downward dressing spiral." According to Wolfe, the fashion industry "pretends it's a positive thing" but he "thinks we're close to the bottom" and may "start looking upward for fashion inspiration again."

For Wolfe (1998) the shift in the latter half of the twentieth century toward an anything-goes-anywhere way of dressing had negative economic consequences for the fashion industry. As he puts it, "If we can redefine appropriate apparel for different occasions, different lives, different ages—we are going to sell a lot more. I think we are going to see people reestablishing some rules because it is too difficult to get dressed in the morning if you don't have rules. Rules make it easier, not harder." That doesn't mean that consumers will give up comfort and casual clothes, but he thinks fashion is "starting to chart a trend toward dressing up again—back toward not uncomfortable formality but appropriateness."

● ● PROFILE (CONTINUED)

As for trends, Wolfe (1999) thinks they work differently now. When he started in the business, "all you had to do was pick out the right person to copy." In those times a trend started as an idea "and it rippled out, and rippled out, and rippled out, and eventually everybody made a bit of money from it." Today he divides trends into "macro" and "micro" categories. "Macro trends are the big, big ideas that affect everybody, in every walk of life, in every price point, every gender—those are the big deals, the real trends." The micro trends are "those cute little ideas that fashion editors love, and fashion stylists love, and the display people love—because they are a great way to communicate excitement to each other in the fashion industry, to get our ideas across." Because of the short life span of these micro trends, people in the industry can make "a little bit of money, intensely for a very, very short period of time, but a nanosecond later, it's over."

As a forecaster, Wolfe (1999) goes back to look at the forecasts he made a decade before to see how things actually worked out. "At the beginning of the 1990s, I said the decade is going to be all about marketing, not about design at all." Looking forward, Wolfe predicted the next decade would be all about technology and the way "it is going to change not just the world of fashion, the world of style, but our world in general." Technology will change what clothes are made from (like high-performance fabrics), the way clothes are made (laser cutouts for decoration and fused seams rather than sewn), clothes themselves (pockets designed for take-along electronic gadgets), and the way the industry communicates with the customer (pinpointing individual customers with electronic messages about new merchandise).

In the mid-2000s Wolfe declared, "There is no fashion mainstream anymore. Instead of mainstream there are a thousand little branches all going at different speeds. It's almost as if the consumer has become a solo player in the marketplace. And that makes it hard to plan mass movements of merchandise" (Horyn, 2005). For the future he forecast (Moin, 2006):

• Electronic gadgets as status-brand luxury accessories.
• Shopping vacations that include the experiences of a spa or cruise.
• A less influential role for the avant-garde.
• Runway shows as entertainment events with ticket sales.
• A "Walden Pond" aesthetic where consumers buy fewer products and only those with timeless quality.

Encouraged by televised fashion shows, reality shows like *Project Runway*, and museum displays of Paris collections, Wolfe sees the public's interest in fashion insider information growing in much the way people became fascinated with show business information in the 1990s (Poggi, 2007).

clothes appreciated by only the most intellectual of the fashion insiders, but they exert tremendous influence on other designers following their lead. Suzy Menkes (2003, 2008b), fashion doyenne of the *International Herald Tribune*, pointed out one such designer: Azzedine Alaia. She challenged observers to "take any look at the collection that the designer showed in Paris in January and you could find its double offered for the autumn-winter season" on other runways. Whether it is "homage or just copycat designing," Menkes sees the designer as exceptionally influential for other designers.

Trial Balloons

Each collection and each season is a learning experience for a designer. The designer sends out a collection and gets feedback from the press, the professional buyers, and the clients. Plans for the next collection mix design influences, the response to the designer's most recent collections, and the reaction of press and merchants to the most recent collections of other designers.

Couture designers are in the business of innovation but ideas evolve over time. Revolutionary revisions like Dior's New Look in 1947 and Courrèges' future-oriented modernism in the 1965 collection are rare. Instead, new fashions first make their appearance as trial balloons, as tentative explorations of a new direction or a new look. Couture is a low-risk way to try out an idea and to judge the reaction because the designer makes only one sample for the runway and custom makes any that sell rather than committing to larger-scale production (Freeman, 2002). When Yvan Mispelaere, couture designer for Féraud, showed girlish collections, his ideas did not catch on except

with Marc Jacobs, who showed very similar looks the season after. Part of the pressure to copy comes from the necessity to produce several collections a year—a pressure that translates into finding ideas wherever a designer can (Horyn, 2001).

When an idea debuts, the designer more fully exploits the new approach in subsequent collections. Meanwhile, others have recognized the innovation, transposed it, developed variations, and amplified it. All these modifications are individual acts of creation based on that initial seed. Together they coalesce into a trend recognizable across collections in a given season. These similarities arise because designers must assert their individuality within the constraints of what their competitors are doing and the spirit of the times (Lipovetsky, 1994).

Knockoffs

The designers' aesthetic is translated to lower price points in three ways:

- The **counterfeit**—a close copy passed off as authentic (Figure 7.15).
- The knockoff—a close copy of another company's original but one that does not carry the originator's label.
- An interpretation of the look—an adaptation that attempts to mimic the aesthetics, not copy the style exactly.

Counterfeiting is big business and is increasing exponentially according to the Counterfeiting Luxury Report conducted by the UK legal firm Davenport Lyons. About one-third of buyers believed the fake to be real, two-thirds were proud to have bought fakes and were willing to boast about it to friends and family—a worrying shift in consumer behavior. Counterfeiting,

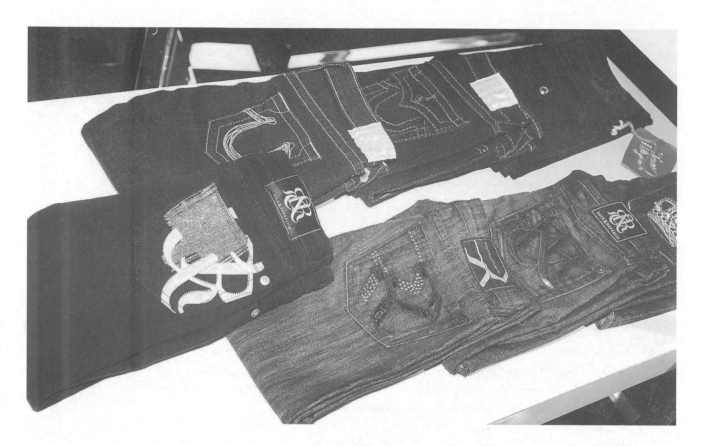

a crime of theft, also damages company reputation, affects sales, and reduces the value of intellectual property like trademarks ("Analysis," 2007).

Direct transmission of runway shows, digital photography, the Internet, and other new technologies are making the job of the counterfeiter easier (Murphy, 2000).

Copying is a deeply ingrained historical practice in the fashion industry. An article in the *Saturday Evening Post* from 1963 states flatly that design "piracy is not the exception in the industry, it dominates it" and illustrates the point with a running industry gag, "At least I changed the buttons" (Poling, 1963). Some designers, even those with big names, copy other designers (Agins, 1994b). Ralph Lauren was found guilty and fined by a French commercial court for "counterfeiting" a long, sleeveless tuxedo dress from Yves Saint Laurent's Fall 1992 couture collection (Betts, 1994; Ingrassia, 1994). Legal cases are being

brought to protect ownership of the way a product looks or is presented under the definition of **trade dress,** a form of trademark infringement (Young, 1998). In these cases, the firm with an original design is attempting to prevent others from trading on its reputation, image, and customer's goodwill by presenting similar goods. Trade dress is an expansion of the trademark law that refers to the design or appearance of a good or service. However, these cases are hard to win when the product is apparel. When a children's clothing manufacturer sued Wal-Mart for copying its line using trade dress, they lost because they could not prove that consumers connected the distinctive look of their line with its origin (their company) (Davczyk, 2000). Trademark law grants use of a particular mark to identify a particular company and its products. Ownership of a trademark is justified because it minimizes consumer confusion about the origin of a product and preserves the goodwill the

Figure 7.15.
Counterfeit copies of branded products deceive customers with low quality and undermine the reputation and profits of the manufacturers who created demand in the first place.
(*WWD,* Courtesy of Fairchild Publications)

Figure 7.16.
Even small-business
entrepreneurs, such as
designers and
boutique owners,
can be targets for
knockoffs.
(*WWD*, Courtesy of
Fairchild Publications)

company has established with that consumer. A word, term, symbol, or device can be trademarked.

The design for Levi's pocket, first trademarked more than 100 years ago, has become the front line for legal battles. The company has filed more trademark infringement lawsuits than any other large corporation in order to remove copies from stores (Barbaro & Creswell, 2007).

For companies that specialize in knockoffs—the translation of high-priced fashion into cheaper versions—technology has speeded up the process. Simonia Fashion, founded in 1980, is one of hundreds of companies copying runway looks for fast-fashion retailers. Seema Anand selects a look from the shows covered online at Style.com, e-mails the picture to her factory in Jaipur, India, and delivers the knockoff months ahead of the designer version (sometimes in as little as 14 days). The company maintains a showroom in New York and has sales of $20 million, about 80 percent in knockoffs for private labels for department stores like Bloomingdale's and Macy's and chains like Forever 21 (Wilson, 2007b).

Runway designers aren't the only ones being knocked off. Dana Foley and Anna Corinna started their partnership as sellers at a flea market and turned their eye for updating vintage into a fashion company with a store on the Lower East Side in New York and one on Melrose Avenue in Los Angeles and $20 million annual sales. When Paris Hilton wore a Foley & Corinna flowery dress (price: $400) on *David Letterman* a fast-fashion chain began selling a $40 copy. The designers went from "under the radar" to publicized for being knocked off—not a plus when customers returned originals, preferring instead the copies (Figure 7.16). What can these entrepreneurs do? Nothing legally since clothing designs are not protected as intellectual property. "We would kick people out of the store who we knew were knocking us off," Ms. Foley said. "One guy spit at Anna's feet when she wouldn't let him buy a dress. He said, 'But I could copy Marc Jacobs!'—like it was a compliment" (Wilson, 2008a).

Top designers like Nicole Miller and Diane von Furstenberg, president of the Council of Fashion Designers of America (CFDA), are working with lawmakers to amend copyright laws to provide three years protection for designs of apparel, handbags, footwear, belts, and eyeglass frames and would establish penalties for those who copy (Ellis, 2007), an effort backed by the American Bar Association (Lynch, 2008). The problem is how to define knockoffs versus trends (looks seen everywhere simultaneously, which are in the public domain). Further blurring occurred when name designers created "cheap chic collections" for mass marketers and fast-fashion chains (Wilson, 2007d). Although most players agree that original ideas deserve protection, designers and manufacturers disagree on how to do it. Manufacturers expect higher costs for research into design ownership, higher legal fees, and delays delivering apparel to stores (Wilson, 2008b). But for designers, timing is the key issue—when knockoffs of potentially best-selling designs arrive in retail stores before the designers' own creations, they lose sales.

TREND DYNAMICS: LABEL, COATTAIL, AND FLOW

Of the many ideas on the runway, only a few are successful in attracting backing. In the first 100 years of modern fashion, this backing came from clients. Some fashion counts from that period show that only one-tenth of the designs were produced for clients (Lipovetsky, 1994). The rest were neglected, forgotten, and replaced by a new crop of proposed fashion ideas in the next season. The gatekeeper role initially played by clients was taken over by merchants and by the fashion press. Merchants decide which fashion ideas will be available to consumers, which will be made in small numbers, and which in volume. The fashion press defines trends by deciding which of the many ideas on the runway will be promoted in the pages of trade publications, newspapers, and fashion magazines.

In the past, collections could be categorized as either "editorial" (providing a hook for telling a story or creating a fantasy) or "retail" (wearable, targeted for a consumer segment). Now the press and the merchants tend to be in sync on the looks that will be tested further in the marketplace (Socha, 1998b). Editors know that readers buy from the pages of the magazine and that everything shown must be available at retail price. Both magazines and stores cover established designers and new talents. More than ever, editors and store executives share information—key fashion stores invite editors to see what they are buying and creating in private-label merchandise for

● ● ● ACTIVITY 7.11. Charting Fashion Labels

Using highlighter pens, identify labels attached to trends, apparel items, and fashion looks in a recent fashion magazine. Develop a dictionary of names, labels, or slogans associated with current fashion in a notebook. Jot down additional ones as you read fashion magazines from now on. Over time, this dictionary of fashion labels will chart the emergence, diffusion, dominance, and eclipse of fashion trends.

a season, and store fashion directors carefully analyze the press' approach. Designers have to be realistic about appealing to both the needs of retailers and the press.

Trends, after identified, must be given a name, label, or slogan that can be used as a popular identifier (Meyersohn & Katz, 1957). If the name is synchronous with the spirit of the times, original, and catchy, it will speed the trend on its way. With the labeling comes a surge in interest. This surge of interest catches the attention of people in the industry who recognize the potential of the trend and rush to produce it in their own lines. This phenomenon is called the coattail effect. Popular at first with a relatively small sphere of "fashionistas," the trend will pass from group to group across social boundaries of age, income, and lifestyle—a process called flow.

TREND ANALYSIS AND SYNTHESIS

Many variations of apparel styles are available in the marketplace simultaneously. Almost all are "marked" with meaning. An unmarked apparel item is the most generic of its kind. When color or styling is added, the apparel becomes a marker for some identity. Think of a white T-shirt. How many meanings can be attached to a simple white T-shirt depending on the way it is worn, its fit, what it is paired with, and the occasion when it is worn? People are symbol users and apparel offers a stage for that ability.

Each person—female or male—must make decisions about what styles to pluck from the marketplace for personal use. These decisions include those about hair, cosmetics, clothing, and accessories. Being antifashion or no-fashion is as much a decision as being fashionable. People make these decisions every day when they dress. Because the decisions are based

partly on demographics, lifestyle, and situation and partly on personality and taste, a certain consistency emerges for each individual—a personal signature style.

People in all likelihood are a member of a style tribe because of where they live, how they make a living, or how they choose to spend their leisure time. Groups evolve a way of dressing that signals the group's identity and aesthetic code.

Because there exists an almost infinite universe of style variations, the possibilities for individual expression and group identification are also infinite. Yet, people's styles can be classified into general categories. Combining styles under an umbrella definition makes it possible for designers to act as style tribe leaders, specialty stores to develop retail concepts that appeal to certain customers and not to others, and marketers to target specific consumer audiences. Marketers call these classification schemes **consumer segmentation** (see Chapters 2 and 8).

Analysis and synthesis are the two faces of forecasting. In **analysis,** a phenomenon is dissected to achieve a more complete understanding of its components. **Synthesis** is a creative reintegration of the parts. In fashion forecasting that means:

- An accurate reading of the trend in all its subtle aspects.
- Matching the trend with the consumer profiles most likely to adopt it initially.
- Matching the trend with the product category, price point, and retail concept most likely to complement it.

Finally, the forecaster hypothesizes about what it will take to energize and accelerate the flow of the trend across consumer segments.

Key Terms and Concepts

Abstracting

Analysis

Consumer segmentation

Core concept

Counterfeit

Designer ready-to-wear

Fashion weeks

Haute couture

Modernity

Muse

Postmodern(ism)

Regional markets

Runway shows

Showrooms

Style tribe

Synthesis

Trade dress

Trade shows

Visual core concept

● CASE REVISITED
From Catwalk to Main Street

As fashion director for a 16-store chain in the midwestern United States, Karla translates the seasonal fashion story into merchandise (purchased from manufacturer's lines and the chain's own private-label operation) targeted for a young, fashion-forward customer. Use the following questions to review and summarize Karla's approach.

Information gathering via travel: Karla does not have a large budget for travel, but she can make one trip to Europe and two trips within the United States. When should she go? What should she plan to accomplish on these trips?

Information gathering on the desktop: To augment her travel, what subscriptions should Karla have? What part should television play in her information gathering? How can she use the Internet in her information gathering?

Merchandising the store:

- The stores need a constant influx of merchandise to keep the look fresh and exciting but the selling floor mustn't look disorganized. How can both requirements be met?
- The stores use a lifestyle concept carrying everything from casual clothes to prom dresses. How can Karla use trend merchandising in each of these categories?

Additional Forecasting Activities

Location, Location, Location. Fashion forecasting services cover the season's styles and then prepare trend books for their clients. These trend books forecast fashion's general direction and make specific suggestions for target audiences. For a given selling season, develop a trend book specifically for your region of the United States.

Systematic Updates. Develop a "bookmark" list of Web sites related to fashion—sites on designers and their collections, online fashion magazines, sites promoting trade shows, blogs, and sites associated with fashion reporting (see Research Pointers for suggestions). Group the sites according to when they are updated—daily, weekly, monthly.

Monitor these sites for three months on a regular basis. Evaluate the costs in terms of time and the payoff in terms of increased knowledge of fashion and trend identification.

What's a Copy? Monitor fashionista.com and counterfeitchic.com for reports of knockoffs. Both sites feature side-by-side photographs of originals and copies. What defines an original? How can it be described in obtaining (future) copyright protection? Develop a set of guidelines for designers, lawmakers, manufacturers, and retailers to use in identifying original designs in apparel, handbags, footwear, belts, and eyeglass frames.

Resource Pointers

These sites on the Web show runway fashion:
www.firstview.com
www.style.com/vogue
www.WWD.com
New York Times: www.nytimes.com/pages/
    fashion/index.html
On the Runway (Cathy Horyn blog)
The Moment (fashion, design, food, travel blog)

These sites feature online-only fashion magazines:
www.lucire.com
www.hintmag.com
www.zoozoom.com

Edited fashion news Web sites:
Fashion TV: www.fashiontelevision.com
Video fashion: www.videofashion.com

For industry calendars, check these sites:
www.mbfashionweek.com
www.infomat.com

Fashion blogs for streetwear:
Fashionista: www.fashionista.com
Street Peeper: www.streetpeeper.com
The Sartorialist: www.thesartorialist.blogspot.com
Bookmarking and social shopping:
    Style Hive: www.stylehive.com

Fashion search engines:
ShopStyle: www.shopstyle.com
Style Hunter: www.stylehunter.com

Portals for fashion information:
Fashion Week Daily: www.fashionweekdaily.com
www.fashion.com
www.fashioninformation.com
Fashion Infomat: www.infomat.com

Note: For vintage clothing sites, see Resource Pointers in
    Chapter 3.